Cultural Resource Management

Cultural Resource Management

A Collaborative Primer for Archaeologists

Edited by

Thomas F. King

In collaboration with Kolawole Adekola, Caitlin Allen,
Jaime J. Awe, Jaime Lynn Bach, Katherine Bracken Ward,
Nancy Farrell, Jay W. Gray, Rebecca A. Hawkins,
Dawn Johnson, Raimund Karl, Hannah Mattson,
Fred L. McGhee, Jason Nez, and Wang Renyu

berghahn
NEW YORK · OXFORD
www.berghahnbooks.com

First published in 2020 by

Berghahn Books

www.berghahnbooks.com

© 2020 Thomas F. King

Library of Congress Cataloging-in-Publication Data

A C.I.P. cataloging record is available from the Library of Congress
Library of Congress Cataloging in Publication Control Number: 2019042647

British Library Cataloguing in Publication Data

A catalogue record for this book is available from the British Library.

ISBN 978-1-78920-623-4 hardback
ISBN 978-1-78920-652-4 paperback
ISBN 978-1-78920-624-1 ebook

To all dugongs, physical and metaphorical, and their human collaborators

Contents

—∿∿—

Preface   ix

Introduction to Cultural Resource Management in the United States   xi

List of Abbreviations   xvi

1.   What Is CRM? How Does it Differ from Archaeology?   1

2.   What CRM Archaeologists Do: Consultation and Identification   24

3.   What CRM Archaeologists Do: Evaluation   40

4.   What CRM Archaeologists Do: Assessing Adverse Effects   62

5.   What CRM Archaeologists Do: Resolving Adverse Effects   73

6.   What Else Do CRM Archaeologists Do?   87

7.   Special Cases and Loose Ends   101

8.   Examples of Worldwide Cultural Resource/Heritage Management   111

    Archaeology and CRM in Australia   111
    Caitlin Allen

    Cultural Resource Management in Belize   117
    Jaime J. Awe

    A Very Brief Introduction to China's *Wenwu* Management
    System and CRM Archaeology   125
    Wang Renyu

CRM in Europe   127
    Raimund Karl

CRM in Nigeria   133
    Kolawole Adekola

9. Thoughts in Conclusion   138

Appendix: Legal Matters   143

About the Author and Collaborators   147

Index   149

Preface

—〰—

Cultural resource management (CRM) is the largest employer of archaeologists in the United States. It also employs many historians, architectural historians, and other specialists in the social sciences and humanities. Under other names—"historic preservation," "heritage protection," "heritage resource management," "cultural heritage," and just plain "heritage" being the most common—and within diverse legal and administrative systems, something like CRM is practiced in most developed nations.

Yet few academic institutions expose their students to the theory and practice of CRM. It seems to be assumed that if one is a well-educated—or even not so well-educated—archaeologist, historian, or architectural historian, one will be prepared to do CRM.

I think this is misguided and counterproductive, because CRM is *not* just a kind of archaeology or history or architectural history or historical architecture. It's more than all that, and different. The name has meaning: CRM involves *managing* those parts of the environment that people think are *resources* because of their *culture*, regardless of what an archaeologist or other specialist thinks of them.

I've published ten books and a lot of journal articles about CRM, and for the last 20 years I've maintained a worldwide weblog on the subject (crmplus. blogspot.com/). None of this, as far as I can tell, has accomplished much. But now, having pretty much used up the time allotted to me in this incarnation, I can't resist putting together one more book—this one designed to speak particularly to archaeologists and their institutions about what I think CRM actually is, and opining about how a responsible archaeologist should do it.

This book is meant to be a shortish, relatively uncomplicated introduction to CRM for archaeologists. It largely reflects my thinking and the fruits (however sour) of my fifty-plus years of experience, but because I don't pretend to "know it all," I asked for help from colleagues, 14 of whom agreed to assist. Nine are CRM archaeologists working in different parts of the United States, who agreed to help make sure that what I've written is relevant to their areas of practice. Five work outside this country—Kolawole Adekola in Nigeria, Caitlin Allen in Australia, Jaime Awe in Belize, Raimund Karl in Europe, and Wang Renyu in China—and have been kind (and masochistic) enough to review the manuscript and provide short essays in chapter 8 outlining how what I've described compares with the way CRM (under whatever name) is done in their parts of the world.

As the book has come together, I've been embarrassed at how complex and bureaucratic its portrayal is of CRM. This is the reality in the United States, and while it would be fruitful to think hard about why that's so, I'd be doing readers a disservice if I portrayed CRM as simpler or less turgid than it is. Things are different in other parts of the world, but this doesn't necessarily make them better (or worse).

— • —

I expect this to be my last book on CRM. I hope readers will find it useful and at least mildly interesting. If anyone wants to correspond about its content, I expect to be at tomking106@gmail.com until the most vulnerable part of my body gives out.

Introduction to Cultural Resource Management in the United States

—m—

Especially for readers outside the United States,[1] but also for those of us within its borders who may not think much about such things in the course of our day-to-day work, here's some context on cultural resource management (CRM) as it's practiced in this country.

A Capitalist Democratic Republic

First, at least in theory, the United States is a democratic republic, in which power derived from the people is distributed among the federal government and the fifty states, the 3,000-plus counties, and the 4,000-plus cities. Several territories (e.g., Guam) and members of the United States commonwealth (e.g., Puerto Rico) unenviably exist in a sort of quasi-state condition. Indian tribes—provided they're recognized by the federal government—are theoretically sovereign and legally superior to the states, but there's a considerable distance between theory and practice.

For better or worse, the United States is deeply committed to private property rights and is rather aggressively capitalistic. In recent decades, this orientation has come into conflict with the need to protect the environment, including its cultural aspects. We have no good way to resolve this conflict; instead, we cobble together compromises. Our environmental and cultural resource laws are such compromises. There is no explicit provision for such laws in our Constitution.

Who Owns What

The land area of the United States comprises almost 10 million square kilometers; if submerged lands on the continental shelf are considered, it's much bigger. Approximately 63 percent of its dry land is privately owned by individuals, families, and corporations. Few, if any, constraints are placed on how such landowners use their lands or what lies within or stands on them, though local governments (cities and counties and their equivalents under other names) and to some extent states do impose varying kinds of zoning and planning controls, sometimes oriented toward protecting the environment.

Let's be very clear about that business of "few, if any, constraints," because it bothers a lot of people in other countries—and in the United States, for that matter. The bottom line is that as far as federal law is concerned, if I have a "cultural resource" on my private property—let's say it's a seventeenth-century manor house containing a 10,000-year-old baked clay idol of an ancient Native American deity—I can with perfect legality tear the building down and grind up the idol for grit to feed my chickens. State or local law may stop me, or my neighbors may do so by force of arms, but federal law won't. That may be wrong, it may be shocking, but there it is.

About 6 percent of land in the country is controlled directly by state governments and is subject to whatever environmental, land use, and cultural resource laws such governments may enact. Some state laws apply to private lands as well. Some local governments and intergovernmental bodies have CRM or CRM-like programs and impose controls on private property owners.

Indian tribes have managed to hold on to about 5 percent of the lands they once occupied and used. Some of these lands are owned outright by tribes, some are held in trust for tribes by the federal government (the Department of the Interior) and make up the bulk of most Indian reservations, and some have been allotted by the Feds to individual tribal members, who hold them more or less as private property. Federal environmental and cultural resource laws in theory apply to most tribal land, as do laws enacted by tribal governments. Some tribes have rights to use land and waters outside the boundaries of their reservations, under the typically ambiguous terms of treaties with the federal government.

About 26 percent of dry land in the United States is controlled directly by the federal government. Most of this land is in the western parts of the country. Most is administered by agencies of the Departments of Agriculture and Interior, although the Departments of Defense, Energy, and Veterans Affairs also have large landholdings.

Landholdings in Alaska are peculiar in that the United States, after purchasing the peninsula from Russia in 1867 (without concern for native title), turned much of its land over to the state and to "native corporations," under the Alaska Native Claims Settlement Act of 1971.

Submerged lands on the continental shelves are mostly under federal jurisdiction, while those under bays, lakes, rivers, creeks, streams, and ponds may be controlled by state, tribal, and local governments, corporate interests, and individuals as well. Generally, environmental and cultural resource laws apply to such lands, but exactly which ones apply, and how, can be pretty ambiguous.

Where Most CRM Work Is Done

The ways in which things like CRM are done in the United States vary widely depending on location. For the most part, CRM work doesn't get carried out *at all* unless there is some involvement by the federal government. There are states like California and territories like Guam with laws that mimic those of the federal government, but most state and territorial laws are a lot weaker, or at least a lot more vague, than those at the federal level. So on the whole, CRM work is done only if the Feds are somehow involved—that is, either on the 31 percent of the land mass (plus submerged land) that's federally owned or held in trust for tribes, or on state, local, or private land where a federal agency is funding a project or is authorized by law to grant or deny a permit.

That actually covers a lot of ground, however. It's a rare large project—highway, reservoir, or power generation scheme, for instance—that doesn't have some federal involvement, no matter whose land is involved.

The National Register

Since 1966, when Congress enacted the National Historic Preservation Act (NHPA), CRM in the United States has been greatly influenced by having a National Register of Historic Places (NRHP). The NRHP is a list of places—pieces of real estate, for the most part—thought to be significant in American history, architecture, engineering, archaeology, and/or culture. The NRHP is maintained by the National Park Service. Anybody can nominate a place to be included in the list, but the process for doing so has become more and more complicated, bureaucratic, politicized, and nitpicky over the decades. Since the early 1970s, thanks to President Richard Nixon, federal agencies have been responsible for considering the effects of their plans and actions not only on places *included* in the NRHP but also on those *eligible* for inclusion. As a result, most CRM work in the United States is built around finding, evaluating, and managing places that are eligible for the NRHP. I'm sorry to say that I'll have a lot more to say about this rather tedious topic.

Where Does the Money Come From?

Unlike many countries, the United States has no central ministry of culture through which money flows to conduct CRM. Most funding for CRM comes from the following sources.

Agency Budgets

Federal agencies, and some state and local ones, budget for the CRM work they expect to do in the course of each fiscal year. This is usually part of a larger

budget designed to support maintaining and operating buildings and installations, managing land, and carrying out projects and programs authorized
by Congress. The agencies responsible for overseeing compliance with CRM
laws—the Advisory Council on Historic Preservation (ACHP) and the National
Park Service (NPS)—also prepare and submit budgets, as does the NPS for
management of the resources it controls and interprets for the public. If Congress approves an agency's budget, CRM is then funded in accordance with
whatever Congress has approved. Each state, tribe, and local government either
budgets similarly for the CRM activities of its agencies, or does not.

Grants

Some United States laws authorize grants to support CRM work. For example, the costs of administering certain state, tribal, and local historic preservation programs (particularly by State and Tribal Historic Preservation
Officers) are partly defrayed by grants from the NPS. Some states also have
grant programs.

Tax Breaks

Since the late 1970s, the notoriously difficult and ever-changing United
States tax code has provided incentives to people who own or develop certain kinds of cultural resources (e.g., historic buildings and structures) to
preserve them and keep them in productive use. Many architectural historians and historical architects make their living by helping property owners
and developers use the tax code. Few archaeologists are involved in this sort
of CRM, and it's always been marginal to my own practice, so I've not dealt
with it in this book.

Compliance

Agencies of the United States government, when planning things like construction and land-use projects, have to comply with laws and regulations
aimed at assessing and controlling environmental impacts. Compliance usually requires conducting studies to identify environmental variables that may
be affected by whatever is being proposed. These studies typically include
CRM work. Compliance often generates the need to mitigate the impacts of
approved projects. The costs of environmental impact assessment and mitigation are routinely passed on to whatever non-federal or non-governmental
parties are authorized to carry out projects—to build roads, to put in power
plants, to develop housing projects, and so on. Compliance is probably the
biggest rationale for CRM work done by archaeologists in the United States,
and it generates most of CRM's funding. Compliance with their own policies
and procedures results in funding for international CRM by the World Bank

and the Agency for International Development, as well as by the United States Departments of Defense and State.

For better or for worse, this book is mostly about compliance-driven CRM—in which I've spent my career.

Note

1. Thanks to Wang Renyu for alerting me to the need for this background.

Abbreviations

A&E	Architect and engineer
ACHP	Advisory Council on Historic Preservation
ACRA	American Cultural Resources Association
AIA	Archaeological impact assessment
APE	Area(s) of potential effects
ARPA	Archaeological Resources Protection Act
BLM	Bureau of Land Management
CBD	Commerce Business Daily
CEQ	Council on Environmental Quality
CEQA	California Environmental Quality Act
COTR	Contracting officer's technical representative
CRM	Cultural resource management
DHS	Department of Homeland Security
DOD	Department of Defense
DOE	Department of Energy
DOI	Department of the Interior
EA	Environmental assessment
EIA	Environmental impact assessment
EIS	Environmental impact statement
FAR	Federal Acquisition Regulation
FEMA	Federal Emergency Management Agency
FERC	Federal Energy Regulatory Commission
FPIC	Free, prior, and informed consent
FWS	Fish and Wildlife Service
GSA	General Services Administration
HABS	Historic American Buildings Survey
HAER	Historic American Engineering Record
HALS	Historic American Landscapes Survey
ICOMOS	International Council on Monuments and Sites

LLC	Limited liability company
MOA	Memorandum of Agreement
MOU	Memorandum of Understanding
NAGPRA	Native American Graves Protection and Repatriation Act
NDA	Non-disclosure agreement
NEPA	National Environmental Policy Act
NGO	Non-governmental organization
NHPA	National Historic Preservation Act
NPI	National Preservation Institute
NPS	National Park Service
NRHP	National Register of Historic Places
OMB	Office of Management and Budget
PA	Programmatic agreement
PC	Program comment
RFP	Request for proposals
RFQ	Request for quotes
SHPO	State Historic Preservation Officer
TCP	Traditional cultural place
TEK	Traditional ecological knowledge
THPO	Tribal Historic Preservation Officer
UNDRIP	United Nations Declaration on the Rights of Indigenous Peoples
UNESCO	United Nations Educational, Scientific and Cultural Organization
USC	United States Code
USDA	United States Department of Agriculture
VA	Department of Veterans Affairs
WHC	World Heritage Convention
WHL	World Heritage List

Chapter 1

What Is CRM? How Does It Differ from Archaeology?

"Cultural resource management." It's a pretty obscure term. What is a "cultural resource," and how does one go about "managing" it? The Merriam-Webster Online Dictionary defines "cultural" as "of or relating to culture or culturing," which isn't very helpful, but it goes on to define "culture" as "the integrated pattern of human knowledge, belief, and behavior that depends upon the capacity for learning and transmitting knowledge to succeeding generations," and as "the customary beliefs, social forms, and material traits of a racial, religious, or social group." So it's safe to say—and this is consistent with what many of us were taught in college anthropology courses—that "culture" is the integrated pattern of a group's knowledge, belief, and behavior, passed on from generation to generation.

"Management," the same dictionary tells us, is "the act or art of … conducting or supervising … something." So a cultural resource manager—a practitioner of cultural resource management—must conduct or supervise an integrated pattern of human knowledge, belief, and behavior, or a set of customary beliefs, social forms, and material traits. Right?

Well, no, not exactly.

Where CRM Came From

To the best of my knowledge, the term "cultural resource management" (which I'll call CRM for short, despite the danger of confusion with "customer relations management," a whole different thing), was dreamed up in the mid-1970s by archaeologists in the southwestern United States, to describe what they (we) were doing in response to a couple of then new United States laws—the

National Environmental Policy Act (NEPA) and the National Historic Preservation Act (NHPA).

Remember those acronyms—NEPA and NHPA! You'll be seeing them a lot. I realize that they aren't directly relevant to readers outside the United States, though, so as we go along I'll try to keep other legal systems—often quite different from ours—in mind. But I have to assume that this book will be read mostly in the United States, where the NEPA and the NHPA structure the practice of CRM. There are also laws called the Native American Graves Protection and Repatriation Act (NAGPRA) and the Archaeological Resources Protection Act (ARPA) that are important in some contexts, and I'll refer to them and other laws from time to time (see also the appendix). But the NEPA and NHPA are the ones with which most CRM archaeologists deal most of the time. Except in California, where the California Environmental Quality Act (CEQA) is dominant, but CEQA would require another whole book to spell out its peculiarities.

The archaeologists who invented CRM—I was among them—were also promoters of another law, enacted in 1974 and variously called the "Archaeological and Historic Preservation Act," the "Archaeological Data Protection Act," and the "Moss-Bennett Act" (after its sponsors). That law is on the books but has never been systematically implemented, so there isn't much to say about it.

The NEPA and NHPA are summarized in this book's appendix. The NEPA generally requires that federal government agencies consider the likely effects of their proposed activities (like building highways, licensing development projects, managing land) on the environment, including its cultural aspects. The NHPA requires that they attend to impacts on "historic properties"—that is, pieces of real estate ("districts, sites, buildings, structures, and objects") included in or eligible for the National Register of Historic Places (NRHP). Section 106 of the NHPA and other sections that support it are the most explicit about this requirement, and the Section 106 regulations[1] structure how most CRM is done in the United States. Both laws—especially the NHPA—have other provisions, but for most CRM practitioners, the requirements laid on government agencies to consider their effects on the environment are the major drivers.

Under the NEPA and NHPA—and in fact under vaguer and more permissive laws that had been around for a decade or more—archaeologists in the 1970s were doing three major things: surveying to find sites worth excavating that were threatened by federal construction projects, excavating these sites, and writing up the results. Doing these things—sometimes with a bow toward trying to keep the sites intact rather than digging them up—was pretty much what we had in mind when we invented CRM. But thinking on this matter has since evolved, as it should.

The term "CRM" has come to be applied not only in the United States, but elsewhere in North and South America, Africa, Australia, Europe, Asia, and the Pacific Islands. As I mentioned in the preface, CRM-equivalent activities outside the United States are often referred to as "heritage resource management," "cultural heritage protection," or simply "heritage."

When United States lawmakers—the senators and congresspeople who passed laws like the NEPA and NHPA—used the word "cultural," they probably had "customary beliefs, social forms, and material traits" (like paintings and opera) in mind. And when they referred to "historic properties," they pretty clearly were thinking about the old buildings, neighborhoods, and battlefields that had traditionally been recognized as "historic" by the National Park Service (NPS). But archaeologists saw a need and filled it. The need was to get better protection for archaeological sites, and it got filled in two ways.

One way was by making sure that archaeological sites were understood by the government to be "historic properties," which, in the United States, meant places eligible for inclusion in the NRHP. The other was to promote attention to archaeological sites in environmental impact studies under the NEPA and its equivalents in other countries. Making both things happen suggested the need for a new and properly pretentious term for the work archaeologists were used to doing, and "cultural resource management" is the term upon which archaeologists in the United States seized.

But, of course, to someone who's *not* an archaeologist, CRM may be taken to mean—well, managing all that cultural stuff, those "customary beliefs, social forms, and material traits" that are out there in the environment, and managing impacts on them. And most people who oversee planning and impact assessment under the NEPA, the NHPA, and the regulations they've spawned, as well as most government agency heads and judges, have at least a fuzzy notion of what "culture" is. To them, as to most ordinary citizens, *it's not just archaeology.*

This has caused a lot of grief over the last 50 years, especially as more and more people and groups who value their "customary beliefs, social forms, and material traits" have become aware of the laws and regulations. Encouraging archaeologists to help resolve this confusion is one reason for this book. A lot of books will teach you about archaeology, but if you think of CRM as only a sort of applied archaeology, you're part of a problem that needs to be fixed.

What CRM Is Supposed to Accomplish

Rather than getting embroiled in abstract arguments about what CRM logically or semantically IS, let's focus on its practicalities. What is it supposed to DO? CRM is practiced mostly in two contexts: in land and resource management and in environmental impact assessment/mitigation.

"Land and resource management" is a pretty large and lumpy bag. It obviously includes managing—taking care of—land, including (but not limited to) land under government ownership or control. It also includes managing what's *on the land*—mountains, lakes, forests, rivers, reservoirs, buildings, cities, highways, parks, military bases, ports, domestic animals and wildlife, fish and shellfish, birds—all of which may be taken to be "resources," as can timber and other plant life growing on the land and minerals lurking beneath it. "Land" may be terrestrial or submerged, so things like shipwrecks on submerged lands are among the things that (sometimes) are managed. "Management" also includes managing what *happens* to land—what's done to it intentionally (see impact assessment, below) and what happens to it through acts of nature, such as fires, floods, earthquakes, erosion, glaciation/deglaciation, and sea level changes, and through human actions that aren't planned by the government, like artifact collecting.

"Environmental impact assessment" (EIA) means getting out in front of a proposed action—construction of a highway, for example, or demolition of a decrepit building—and figuring out how the action, if carried out, may affect the environment. The results of EIA are supposed to inform decision making about whether and how to carry out the action, or some alternative action. EIA often leads to conducting "mitigation" activities—that is, activities designed to avoid, reduce, minimize, or compensate for the damage that an action may have.

There's obviously a lot of overlap between these categories. Impact assessment and mitigation may be done as parts of land and resource management, for example. But generally they're the contexts *in which* CRM is done, and so their purposes are the purposes *for which* CRM is done. CRM is done in order to manage something, or in order to assess and/or mitigate impacts.

Theoretically, the "something" that CRM manages, and upon which it assesses impacts, *ought to be* whatever is "cultural" in the relevant environment—on, in, over, or under the land and/or infrastructure being managed or potentially affected by an action. It is all those "customary beliefs, social forms, and material traits," including *but not limited to* archaeological sites and their contents, and including *but not limited to* "historic properties" as defined under the NHPA. When we define that "something" more narrowly, we deprive some kinds of cultural resources of the consideration the laws afford. This is really important, so let me say it again with emphasis: when we define "cultural resource" as something less than *all* those aspects of the environment valued by people for cultural reasons, *we deprive some kinds of cultural resources of the consideration the laws afford.* Since culture tends to be pretty important to people, that's a pretty big deal.

Who Does CRM?

Because archaeologists invented and first used the term, archaeologists were and continue to be the ones who often wind up doing CRM, either of their own volition or on assignment by employers. Back in the 1970s, most of what came to be called CRM was done by academic archaeologists, but this changed quickly, for several reasons.

Reason One: There was simply too much work. As federal agencies in the United States began to set up the structures to implement the NEPA and NHPA, as state-level equivalents like the California Environmental Quality Act (CEQA) came into force, and as other nations and international bodies established similar systems, it became necessary to do a lot of EIA work—far more than the academic institutions could handle, and often on schedules that just didn't synchronize with academic calendars.

This gap was quickly filled by private-sector interests. Architect and engineer (A&E) consulting firms were among the most aggressive fillers of the void—despite obvious though almost universally ignored conflicts of interest between assessing the impacts of projects and designing or building them. Quite a few independent EIA and CRM companies were also established; most though not all of these have since been gobbled up by the A&E firms.

Reason Two: The organization of EIA work didn't necessarily match the pigeonholes represented by academic departments. Many different disciplines may be involved in CRM, for example. The regulations developed to implement the NEPA explicitly call for *interdisciplinary* research as a basis for EIA. In the 1960s and 1970s, there wasn't always a whole lot of interdisciplinary communication in academia. That may be changing, but if so, the change got underway after EIA/CRM and academia had pretty much parted company.

Here in alphabetical order is a rough—and non-exclusive, please!—list of professional disciplines that are or ought to be involved in CRM:

- Archaeology—Study of the human past with special reference to its physical leavings.
- Architectural history—Study of the history of architectural styles, forms, modes of design and construction, etc. To be distinguished from historical architecture (see below).
- Architecture—Design of buildings, structures, and landscapes.
- Cultural anthropology/ethnography—Study of living human societies, cultures, communities, ways of life, relations with the environment.
- Engineering—Design and construction of machines, mechanical systems, and related structures.
- Geography—Study of the earth's physical characteristics and atmosphere, and of human activity as it affects and is affected by them.
- Historical architecture—Practice of architecture on and in historic buildings and structures, with varying degrees of respect for their integrity.
- History—Study of the human past, usually via the written record or through the recollections of living people (oral history).
- Landscape architecture—Design of landscapes like gardens, parks, and parkways; the study of such design.
- Landscape history—Study of history as embodied or expressed in landscapes.

Reason Three: Many academic institutions took *themselves* out of the CRM and EIA business, not only because they couldn't keep up with the work or couldn't coordinate between departments, but also because they viewed the work itself as too grubby, too compromising, and, in the eyes of many academics, too intellectually undemanding. This has had a couple of unfortunate effects.

One effect is to create a self-fulfilling prophecy. If the institutions treat CRM and EIA practitioners as second-class scholars (or worse), that's the kind of people they route into the work, equipped only with master's degrees (MAs) or even only bachelor's degrees (BAs). And because somebody with an MA or a BA typically can demand less money than someone with a doctorate (usually a PhD), the consulting firms are usually happy to hire them in lieu of someone with heavier-duty academic credentials.

A lot of my best friends—including most of my collaborators in writing this book—don't hold PhDs, and I think they're excellent scholars and responsible CRM practitioners. But they don't have the sort of automatic cachet that comes with a PhD, and more importantly they don't have as many employment options as do those of us whose degrees are "piled higher and deeper." Whether they want to or not, they pretty much have to work in the consulting game, or for the government, or go flip burgers. When a client responds to a report that something important has been found by telling the consultant to "unfind it"—yes, this does happen—the consultant is stuck between a rock and a hard place. It can take a lot of guts to say, in essence, "No sir, I can't do that." And if you say that too often, particularly in a company whose eye is fixed firmly on the financial bottom line or in an agency concerned mostly with institutional survival, it can have serious career implications.

Another effect is to give seeming substance to an untruth. The notion that CRM archaeology is second-class archaeology is not necessarily a responsible or truthful one. Though it's certainly the case that a CRM archaeologist doesn't get to focus her life's work on an abstract research problem or the history of a particular society, locality, or time period, there's nothing that's inherently less intellectually challenging about CRM than about "pure" archaeological research. Assuming purity exists.

And, finally, I suspect that academic institutions may have shot themselves in the foot by effectively tracking CRM practitioners into receiving master's degrees as the endpoints of their academic careers. If one thinks a PhD isn't necessary or desirable in order to feed oneself and one's family, one just might not expend the time and money it takes to get one, and surely this affects the health and welfare of academic institutions.

Jay Gray, a collaborator on this book, tells me that in the eastern United States where he works, increasing numbers of PhDs are going into CRM, and saying it's by choice. Hannah Mattson, another collaborator, reports a similar trend in the southwest. That's precisely the choice I made back in the mid-1970s, and I have seldom regretted it, so I guess I'm cheered by this news. I wonder whether it doesn't say more about the discontent inherent in the academic job market than it does about the attractions of CRM. But still, it may be a positive trend.

In other countries, things are somewhat different. The laws and regulations are different, and in some cases the academic community is much more involved.

This presents its own problems—of bureaucracy, of academic infighting, of narrow-mindedness—but it may avoid some of the problems we've faced (though mostly ignored) but not solved in the United States. However, the United States model is by no means applied only in this country. Similar systems characterize CRM—under whatever name—in several British Commonwealth countries and elsewhere. International entities like the World Bank have also adopted similar systems. As a result, there are A&E firms, with EIA and CRM subsidiaries, working all over the world.

While we archaeologists were creating and expanding our employment niche as CRM experts, other specialists were carving out their own pieces of the action, often using different terms for the overall enterprise in which they were engaged. Applied architectural historians and historical architects tend to identify themselves as engaged in "historic preservation," while some historians specializing in applied work with texts or oral sources call themselves "public historians." A full-service CRM organization will have access to these specialists along with archaeologists, but in smaller operations, archaeologists are likely to be tasked with addressing all kinds of cultural resource issues.

And even if you have a team of archaeologists, historians, and architects of various persuasions, you may still not be equipped to deal with all the aspects of "human knowledge, belief, and behavior," or "customary beliefs, social forms, and material traits" that a chunk of land or bunch of resources may present, or that may be affected by a planned project.

If you don't deal with all these aspects and yet say that what you're doing is "cultural resource management," you're not really telling the truth. Your contract or employer's rules may prohibit you from considering cultural resources other than archaeological sites or old buildings, or from talking with people about their "knowledge, ... customary beliefs, [and] social forms." But if that's the case, you ought to be honest in what you call yourself and what you're doing. You're doing applied archaeology and/or architectural history; you're *not* helping manage the whole universe of cultural resources.

Communities in (and NOT in) CRM

Culture exists in the heads and behaviors of living creatures—notably, though not exclusively, human beings—and it's most clearly exhibited in groups of creatures organized into *communities*.

"Community" is defined—says Merriam-Webster Online—as "a unified body of individuals." Examples given are "the people with common interests living in a particular area," and "a group of people with a common characteristic or interest living together within a larger society" (such as a community of retired persons or a monastic community). Or "a body of persons of common and especially professional interests scattered through a larger society" (such as "the academic community"). There are a couple of other examples, but you get the idea. It's in communities that culture resides, and "cultural resources" are logically the physical, intellectual, and spiritual things that communities more or less share and value.

The laws of most nations are at least ostensibly aimed at protecting and enhancing the lives and welfare of their human citizens. A few enlightened governments concern themselves about non-human "citizens" as well—for instance, India, New Zealand, and other countries have recognized that rivers have legal rights.[2] But generally lawmakers are concerned about the welfare of their voting, taxpaying human constituents, who usually comprise communities. So laws tend to respect the concerns of communities.

This generalization applies to environmental laws like the NEPA and cultural laws like the NHPA, as well as criminal laws and tax codes. So you'd think that human communities would be at the very center of CRM. Theoretically, that's the case, but in practical terms it isn't.

This is partly because it's difficult to involve communities in all the things that are managed by government agencies, that require EIA, and people aren't necessarily very concerned about all of them. Replacing a rusted-out culvert under a road on a National Forest in the United States requires the Forest Service to review its likely impacts. But a LOT of culverts need to be replaced each year, and does anybody really care about the impacts of replacing culvert number 20NO3517B?

Well, yes, sometimes people do—if the culvert is in an indigenous group's ancestral village, or if replacing it is going to alter streamflow in such a way as to mess up fish populations downstream or upstream. But in most cases of culvert replacement, road resurfacing, power pole replacement, and other routine actions, there's not much cause for community concern. There are administrative mechanisms for filtering out the problematic cases from those that are truly "routine."

The more insidious reason that communities are not much involved in CRM is that "professional" practice has excluded them. This goes back to the fact that it was archaeologists who invented CRM, and architectural historians who invented historic preservation. And it was biologists, ecologists, and water/air quality scientists who invented EIA. To all of us "-ologists," what was and is most important is that *we* be involved in data gathering and decision making, and call the shots to the extent possible. So the laws, regulations, and professional practice guidelines all got written to emphasize interaction between agencies and professionals in and (occasionally) outside government. There's usually a bow or two to "community involvement," "public participation," and/or "transparency," but these don't require much beyond sharing paperwork and holding meetings. What people say in such meetings or in response to such paperwork can usually be ignored as long as it's acknowledged somehow.

The "-ologists" who are most skilled at eliciting and working with how people in communities view and value things are cultural anthropologists—who sometimes are labeled or call themselves "sociologists" or "cultural geographers" or "ethnographers." Cultural anthropologists—I'm cherry-picking from Duke University's website here—learn about a community's "structures of symbol, belief, and power." They're especially qualified—at least in theory—to understand how a community relates to its environment, and how it may be affected by a proposed action.

Sadly, not many cultural anthropologists work in CRM—though their numbers are gradually increasing. There are several reasons for their scarcity. For one thing, they're seldom encouraged to get involved by their academic advisors, who tend to think of CRM as a game for archaeologists, and second-rate archaeologists at that. For another thing, many CRM and EIA consulting firms don't recognize that cultural anthropologists could be useful. Why can't archaeologists do the job?

In a sense, this is a good question. In the United States, archaeologists are educated mostly in departments of anthropology, where we're exposed to at least two or three of the discipline's four major subfields—social/cultural, physical/biological, archaeology, and linguistics.[3] In principle, an archaeologist ought to be alert to cultural resources and cultural resource issues that are not strictly archaeological. Some are, but many—too many—aren't. Many of us are simply a lot more comfortable with the dead than with the living, and haven't troubled ourselves to learn much about dealing with the latter.

In my own CRM career, I've had to deal with the following non-archaeological but still very cultural issues, among others:

- Traditional fishing, navigation principles, and spiritual practices in Micronesia
- Cultural attachments to lands in Appalachian American communities
- The cultural significance of fish and fishing on the Colorado, Klamath, and Ch'u'itnu Rivers of Arizona, California, and Alaska
- The origin traditions of the Cahuilla and Luiseño tribes, and of Ojibwe bands
- Dream travel through physical space by the Quechan tribe's spiritual practitioners
- Culturally important marine mammals and their habitats off Okinawa
- Traditional hunting and gathering practices and beliefs in several tribes
- Land-based cultural values of displaced Anglo-American communities in Kentucky, Louisiana, and Texas
- Associations with and beliefs about ancestral remains among Native Americans, Micronesians, and African-Americans
- The traditional importance of wild horses in the southern and western United States
- The interests of military veterans and their families in the places where such veterans receive medical treatment and are buried

Very little I learned as a student and journeyman archaeologist prepared me for the challenges of dealing with such groups, interests, and values, but my training in anthropology did—to some extent. I was greatly assisted—and often challenged—by being married to a cultural anthropologist, the late and much-lamented Pat Parker. Without Pat's guidance and support, I'd have been a whole lot less able to do responsible CRM.

So here's the point. It's easy to interpret laws like the NEPA and the NHPA to require attention only to what you've learned about as a student archaeologist, but if you're doing your job right—if you're paying attention to the whole range of "cultural resources" that people value, and that the laws require you to consider—you're going to have to stretch yourself intellectually and often spiritually. Be bigger than you may have been taught to be as an archaeologist, more open-minded, more considerate of other people, other values, other beliefs.

And try, as a student and as a professional, to *learn* about other cultures. Take classes in cultural anthropology and its key methods. Take classes focused on particular cultural groups, even if they aren't groups in whose archaeology you're interested—but especially and most vitally if they are. Seek out people who belong to such groups and talk with them.

I asked my good friend (but non-relative) Shelly Davis-King—an archaeologist turned ethnographer working in CRM—for her thoughts, and she offered the following recommendations, which I think are on point:

> In many ways the most important thing is to get as much experience and as many contacts with different people and groups as possible. The wider the experience, the greater the ability to open one's mind to new ways of thinking. I can't say my academic training helped me very much at all, but working in pubs and bars, learning how to interview through working on television programs, striking up conversations with strangers in train stations—all these helped. The more I listened to people, the better I got at hearing. That may seem circular, but it's really important.
>
> The time I've spent with American Indian people has been especially important, especially the time we've spent out in the field. I remember when someone showed me a rock and said it was a frog effigy. I had to get out of my own head in order to collect the stone and put it in a bag and call it a frog effigy. Similarly, when I interviewed Portuguese-American people about their Fest Parade ceremony and how it related to the proposed installation of a highway roundabout, I had to listen to what made it better for them, and not impose what I thought was best. That's the most difficult part—getting the whole emic/etic thing right.
>
> Learning another language is a great way to help get yourself to think about things differently. The Inuit really do have something like fifty words for different kinds of snow; if you don't understand them, you can't understand the Inuit environment as they see it. Once a Miwok elder told me that a particular medicine plant was called kitch-en-noo. I asked him what it did, and he told me it kept the spirits at bay. I asked him what the word meant literally; he laughed and said it was like a little coyote/dog sitting on your shoulder giving you guidance. When I looked it up later in a Miwok-English dictionary, it was translated as "little helper." Understanding the term and its context gave me ways to think about that medicine that I could never have gotten just from its botany or even from the way it's described in the literature.

> I guess the bottom line for me is: open your mind to all sorts of experiences, both in school and out. Nothing you do, from what seems like the most menial of tasks to the loftiest of goal-seeking activities, is irrelevant to learning and opening your mind to the great variety of human expression that is culture. Ask questions, be ready to listen, and "rehear" [the term of the pioneer ethnographer John Peabody Harrington] to make sure you garner what is meant.

You're unlikely to get a lot of encouragement from your employers to do what Shelly advises, but if you're going to do your job in a way that will let you be comfortable with yourself when you grow old, you really have to. In CRM, perhaps more than in any other field where archaeologists find employment, *you really have to be an anthropologist first.*

Another reason for thinking anthropologically in CRM is that you're almost inevitably going to be working within some sort of bureaucracy—governmental or corporate, or maybe tribal. Anthropological thinking can help you understand how that bureaucracy works and why it fails to work. If nothing else, this can be personally comforting, and maybe it can be a career enhancer. If you know how the system works, you can perhaps *make* it work, or make it work better. Maybe that will be appreciated. I have to admit, however, that I've never seen much appreciation dumped on those who use anthropology to make systems work for everyone involved.

What all this really comes down to is being respectful—of the people and communities with whom you work, of your employers and clients, of those who regulate what you do, and particularly of people who hold viewpoints different from your own. It's not easy. You may not even know what constitutes respect in a particular context, and missteps are easy to make. But the Golden Rule is a pretty good guide, as is being willing to listen, change your mind, and apologize.

Clients

Among the other people you'll have to deal with are your (or your employer's) clients—the people who pay for your work. The client, understandably, is mainly concerned with how your work and findings, and the time it takes to do the work and arrive at the findings, will affect his or her bottom line. In the United States, and often elsewhere, the client is someone who wants to do something: build a road or a housing project, put in wind generators or a surface mine, cut timber or expand a hospital. The client may want to do this for no reason other than to make money (which, of course, can be a powerful incentive), or may have more admirable motives—to save lives on the highway, to cure the sick in the hospital. In theory, none of that should affect what you do: your job is to assess what impacts may result from whatever is proposed. It's a good idea to be pretty upfront about this. No matter how wonderful the project or activity is that your client proposes, your job is to make a thorough, objective assessment of its impacts. That, in theory, is what the law requires, so it's in your client's best interests (and yours, of course, or your employer's) to let you—indeed, help you—do your job in the best, most honest and honorable way you know how.

BUT—you knew there had to be a "but"—in the United States and other capitalist countries, everybody's struggling to survive, and to climb to the top of the heap. Your clients, if they're a business enterprise, are struggling to make as much money as possible for their owners and shareholders. That's to be expected and to some extent is mandated in law. So they're not likely to be wild about having their project delayed, or being driven to spend more money than expected on some weird "cultural resource" stuff—let alone having their project stopped altogether. They may very well want to do the bare legal minimum—the minimum that they believe is legally required. That, as we'll see, is often pretty minimal. It's also often the subject of a lot of confusion.

Meanwhile, your employers are trying to make good on their contract, and to gain another and another down the road. The last thing they need is to be viewed as the outfit that charges more than is necessary, does more than is necessary, to gain the government approvals that the client seeks. Or worse yet, *not* get them. The result is an inevitable, inexorable spiral to the bottom, a devolution to the lowest common denominator—which tends to be: "Do only what's necessary to satisfy government regulators and keep us out of court."

This might be OK if regulators were vigilant and wise, and if there were a whole lot of knowledgeable, skillful, well-financed litigators prepared to watch-dog every project and challenge those that need challenging. But neither is the case. More about regulators below, but suffice to say that few are well-enough staffed or funded, or immune enough from politics, to be reliable safeguards against sleazy dealing. As for litigation, there has to be someone to do the litigating. Those who might do so—citizens' groups, archaeological societies, environmental organizations—all are congenitally underfunded, understaffed, and often sadly unsophisticated when it comes to the law.

What saves CRM—to the extent it is saved—is that it's usually very small potatoes in the general scheme of a development project. It doesn't cost *that* much; it doesn't hold things up *that* much. So clients find it tolerable most of the time. But not always.

Sometimes CRM actually can get in the way of a project—even a big project with a lot of political muscle behind it. However justified this may be, and despite the fact that it's usually because someone—often the client—failed to do things wisely, the knee-jerk response by clients, their stockholders, and their public relations outfits and lawyers is to blame the regulatory regime and those who profit from it. Like CRM archaeologists.

I know of no simple solution to this problem. We live with it, try to maneuver around it, anticipate and prepare for it. Too often, in my opinion, we let it constrain our honesty and responsibility toward the public and the environment. We ought not do that. Where a real conflict exists, we need to own up to it, talk with our clients about ways to resolve it, and not let them off the hook just because they *are* our clients. I know, easy for *me* to say.

Regulators

A regulatory agency, Wikipedia tells us, is "a public authority or government agency responsible for exercising autonomous authority over some area of human activity in a regulatory or supervisory capacity."[4] One might expect government to set up a general purpose agency to regulate development—to be concerned with all aspects of a highway's or pipeline's or mine's potential environmental impacts as well as its economics, its simple feasibility and necessity, and its other intersections with the public interest. There's no such agency in the United States, although the Army Corps of Engineers is (theoretically) responsible for issuing or withholding permits to discharge fill into United States waters based on the overall public interest.[5] For the most part, the regulatory regime in the United States is a hodgepodge of more or less special-purpose agencies. The Fish and Wildlife Service regulates impacts on threatened and endangered species,[6] for example, and even the seemingly all-purpose Environmental Protection Agency focuses mostly on those aspects of the environment that can be polluted—air and water—with sporadic attention to community environmental justice concerns.[7] There is no regulatory body specifically responsible for concerning itself with cultural resources, though the Council on Environmental Quality (CEQ), which oversees compliance with the NEPA, does call on agencies to be concerned about them.[8]

It is with one particular kind of cultural resource—the "historic property"—that the regulatory regime in the United States especially concerns itself through the operations of specific federal regulations and four semi-regulatory agencies: the Advisory Council on Historic Preservation (ACHP), the State Historic Preservation Officer (SHPO), the Tribal Historic Preservation Officer (THPO), and the National Park Service (NPS). This doesn't mean that cultural resources more broadly defined can be ignored—only that it's easiest to address them if they can be somehow related to the category "historic property."

SHPOs, THPOs, ACHP

Of all the regulators, CRM archaeologists in the United States most often encounter SHPOs. Occasionally, you might need to deal with the ACHP, but since that eventuality is so rare, we needn't discuss it much in this short book. Similarly, you may need to work with a THPO, but that's relatively rare, too. Let's focus on SHPOs, which are not unlike the ministries of culture and similar bodies that oversee CRM in many other countries.

When the NHPA was enacted in 1966, one of its provisions was for the National Park Service (NPS) to provide grants to "state liaison officers" who would coordinate NRHP nominations and other work under the law in each state. These officers evolved into today's SHPOs. Now every state and state-like jurisdiction (District of Columbia, American Samoa, etc.) has one, each with its own range of duties and authorities, all funded in part and loosely overseen by the NPS. One of the SHPO's functions is to participate in project review under NHPA Section 106.

It is widely believed that SHPOs are supposed to "clear" (or presumably not clear) projects—that is, issue go/no-go findings based on the impacts the project is thought likely to have on historic places (or, in some renderings, "cultural resources"). Some SHPOs like this idea and promote it. It's simple, and it gives the SHPO a lot of (perceived) power. Some agencies and project proponents like it too, because it makes things relatively simple. Satisfy the SHPO (or go to your governor and make sure the SHPO is told to be satisfied), and you're all set.

In fact, under the NHPA, the SHPO has neither the authority nor the responsibility to "clear" projects. The federal agency responsible for a project is required to *consult* with the SHPO, and at certain steps in the consultation process the SHPO can say "no" and force the agency to consult with the NPS about the significance of a historic place, or with the ACHP about any potential adverse effects. But it's not a simple matter of issuing or withholding "clearance."

And the SHPO ought to alert the responsible agency that it needs to consult with *other people*—notably Indian tribes, local governments, property owners, and others potentially affected by the project—because the regulations require these people to have the opportunity to participate. This requirement tends to get fuzzed by the belief that SHPO clearance is the centerpiece of Section 106 compliance.

Tribal Historic Preservation Officers (THPOs) have the same general authorities as SHPOs, but within the boundaries of tribal reservations, which are not always the same as the boundaries of land held by or on behalf of the relevant tribe. They may also have other authorities and responsibilities under tribal law, and may participate in reviews under NHPA Section 106 of projects beyond the boundaries of tribal reservations. More and more tribes are establishing THPOs, which helps make sure that tribal perspectives are given voice in consultations under Section 106. But this sometimes creates confusion about just who speaks for a tribe—is it the THPO or is it the tribe's political leadership?[9] Typically, THPOs are even more resource-starved than are SHPOs.

Under some tribal, state, and local laws in the United States, and in some other countries, the SHPO or some equivalent historic preservation body— Preservation Commission, Ministry of Culture, National Museum, Provincial Archaeologist, Historical Resources Ministry—*does* have what amounts to clearance authority, which makes things rather simpler but may deprive other interested parties of the opportunity to influence how decisions are made.

NPS

I listed the NPS among the historic preservation regulators in the United States, but it traditionally denies indulging in anything so nasty as regulating anyone's behavior. Yet (to paraphrase Wikipedia) the NPS does exercise "autonomous authority over certain areas of human activity in a regulatory or supervisory capacity." It supervises the SHPOs and THPOs to some extent, and it regulates access to the NRHP. It's in the latter capacity that most CRM archaeologists most often encounter the NPS, and it's rare. We'll discuss this in chapter 3.

Other Regulators

In the United States, the Army Corps of Engineers, the Coast Guard, the Federal Energy Regulatory Commission, the Fish and Wildlife Service, the Environmental Protection Agency, and others have regulatory functions. So do the big land management agencies like the Bureau of Land Management, the Department of Energy, the National Park Service, and the Forest Service, with respect to land under their control. This can create a pretty complicated situation. The Corps of Engineers, for example, has its own truly weird putative NHPA Section 106 procedures for its regulatory program, called "Appendix C—Procedures for the Protection of Historic Properties."[10] These are virtually nonsensical, but the Corps loves them because it can interpret them to mean whatever pleases those the Corps ostensibly regulates. The Federal Energy Regulatory Commission (FERC) has procedures that are highly structured and quasi-judicial, behind which it hides and generally does nothing except to insist that all the "i's are dotted and t's are crossed" before signing off on whatever's proposed. I've yet to come across a regulatory agency with a clear vision of its public purpose.

Regulators: The Bottom Line

What you need to understand, for now, is that your client, or the government agency to which your client reports, usually has a regulator (or multiple regulators) to whom *they* report. And the regulator or regulators may have a good deal of influence over what the agency or client does and how they do it.

In addition—and this is important to understand—cultural resource-oriented regulators like the SHPO or THPO almost invariably are poorly funded and have relatively little political power. Cultural resources, heritage, historic preservation—all these are nice things. But when push comes to shove, they are not politically high-priority items, and don't get big chunks of the national or state or provincial or tribal economic pie.

Because they don't get big slices of the economic pie, cultural resource regulators in the United States are seldom able to hire the most highly qualified people to populate their cubicles. Here we again run into the problem of the unengaged academic community. Few universities even try to equip their graduates to work in agencies like SHPOs, and some discourage their more promising students from engaging in such work. So cultural resource regulatory offices tend to be staffed by people whose academic credentials are rather thin, and whose alternative job prospects are limited.

This is not to say that there aren't smart, wise, dedicated people in such offices. It's just to say that the system doesn't select for them, so there's a better than even chance that the regulatory staffer with whom you or your employer has to deal won't be one of them. And even if the staffer *is* smart, wise, and dedicated, she or he probably can't risk being fired, because there aren't a lot of other steady jobs out there.

Add to this the fact that regulatory workloads are often enormous. On any given day, the average SHPO staffer in the United States will have anywhere from 10 to 30 or more cases to juggle. "Cases" typically refer to projects needing review under Section 106 of the NHPA. For each of these, the staffer needs to be pretty well-versed on the project's character, its background, its likely impacts, where it stands in the regulatory process, and who's involved in the review—or at least be able to put on a good show of being well-versed. Many cases, of course, are dead simple—the culvert under a Forest Service road sort of thing. But others aren't, even some that seem simple at first glance.

One strategy for handling this variety is to pretend it doesn't exist by treating all cases the same. Set up a standard system and follow it. This can work fairly well much of the time, but it deadens the mind, making one resistant to unusual situations and creative ways of handling them. And if the standard system isn't very carefully designed and managed, it can mask serious issues and fail to flag the culvert under a Forest Service road that's likely to go through an ancient cemetery, for example, or might take out the tree where every lovesick high school boy for the last five generations has carved his sweetheart's initials.

Standard systems, too, often take on lives of their own. So a given regulator's standard system comes to be taken—by that regulator and by those who seek the regulator's blessing—as what the law requires. The standard system may have nothing whatever to do with what the law or regulations require, but that doesn't matter. It's "the way we always do it," and it may come, effectively, to substitute for compliance with law and regulation—until somebody takes somebody to court. But few cases get taken to court, and even when they do, the results are not always enlightening or helpful.

Bottom line: know that the regulators are there and have serious influence over what your employer and/or client does. But don't assume that the regulators know the law and regulations, or have the resources and time to get fully conversant with your project. Or the motivation to care.

Working Directly for the Government

While most CRM archaeologists in the United States work for CRM, EIA, and other kinds of consulting firms, quite a few work directly for government agencies—land management agencies, action agencies, and regulatory agencies. What they do depends mostly on what the agencies that employ them do.

Archaeologists who work for land management agencies may do a fair amount of archaeology, and if they're interested in the areas under the jurisdiction of the offices in which they work, this may be nice work—getting paid to do the kinds of archaeology you like to do, and work on the research questions that interest you. But it's important to remember that the laws do not say "take care of archaeological sites that Sally Shovel thinks are neat," or "spend lots of money doing research that Sally Shovel thinks is important." Laws like the NEPA are intended to protect the public interest in the environment; laws like the NHPA are meant to protect the public interest in places thought to have cultural or historical value—and in a democracy, that means value to *all kinds of people.* The public interest may not coincide precisely with Sally's interests, and things can get particularly problematic if Sally steers a lot of her agency's resources into taking care of places or doing research that interests her at the expense of places and studies that the taxpayers, who ultimately pay her salary, care about.

In fact, though, Sally probably won't have a whole lot of time to promote her own agenda. Most of her time will likely be taken up looking at other, non-archaeological projects that someone proposes on the land she helps manage. Zippyzap Energy wants to put in a power line, Hydrogrow Irrigation wants to put in a reservoir, and the district's public works department has 200 culverts that need to be replaced. Each such project needs to be considered under the NEPA and NHPA. Somebody has to figure out what impacts they may have and what to do about them, which will probably involve doing studies, consulting with regulators and affected people, writing reports, negotiating agreements. That's likely to take up much, if not most, of Sally's time.

Working for an action agency—one that builds or helps build things, like a highway or public works department—also involves mostly reviewing the likely impacts of proposed projects, but in this case they're projects proposed by your own agency, which presents special problems. Although you'll probably be lodged in an "environmental" office whose job it is (in theory) to look critically at each project's potential environmental effects, there will almost always be a strong organizational bias toward being a team player. Widening Highway A-106 between Bigtown and Littleburg is a priority, and everybody on staff is likely to be expected to help make it happen. Needless to say, this can present serious conflicts if there's a really important (to you or somebody else) archaeological site—or old building, or culturally important landscape, plant stand, waterway, or wildlife habitat—in the way.

Working in a regulatory agency means you'll spend your time reviewing the potential impacts of other people's projects that are subject to your agency's authority. In the United States Army Corps of Engineers, this means projects that affect rivers, harbors, waterways, and wetlands, including piers, docks, pipelines, and the like. There are ongoing arguments about the kinds of waters to which the Corps's authorities apply, and about how far those authorities extend *outside* the water. For example, does the Corps have to consider the damage a pipeline will do to an archaeological site a hundred miles from the pipeline's Corps-regulated stream crossing? There's no point in our getting involved in such arguments here.[11] Just understand that they exist and can influence what you do. Every other regulatory agency has its own rules and policies that structure how it regulates, and what its employees can and can't do.

Working for an SHPO or a THPO is comfortable in that you can pretty much focus on "cultural resource" concerns without a whole lot of worry about the other things for which a more general-purpose regulatory body is responsible (endangered species, water quality, etc.). And it may enable you to focus your attention on an area (a state or reservation) in which you have research interests. On the other hand, you'll probably not make a very good living, and your job will forever be at risk. And remember that those "cultural resource" concerns aren't just archaeological concerns. They extend to old buildings, cultural landscapes, traditional cultural places, and—depending on the model of CRM to which your state or tribe subscribes—other cultural resources such as plants, animals, songs, stories, and languages.

In the United States, thanks to Section 106 of the NHPA and its regulations, the SHPO or THPO is a choke point through which all land-use and construction proposals that involve federal land, money, or permits must pass. In some other countries, the equivalent body has similar power over *all* project proposals. This has a couple of tricky results for employees of an SHPO, a THPO, or their equivalent.

For one thing, it can convey the perception of power and produce some of the corruption that real power brings with it. You may be able to enforce your will on some people—notably other archaeologists—by forcing them to do things, say things, or write things the way you want them to. This may be fine up to a point, but carried to extremes, it can make you a petty dictator.

The other thing about your power is that it's illusory. You will inevitably find yourself under pressure to accommodate the *real* power of others—your bureaucratic superiors, higher government officials and legislators, and people who have more economic or political muscle than you have. That's a large crowd of people, unless you've invested a lot of time and trouble in building your own network of high-powered political supporters. You'll be pressured to roll on issues, and you need to be ready to pick the issues on which to roll and on which to fight.

Don't forget, too, that you can expect to be overworked and underpaid; that pretty much goes with the territory.

Study Questions

1. What are the intellectual bases of CRM? What is its underlying logic and its justification?
2. What barriers exist to community involvement in CRM, and what can be done about them?
3. What kind of employment in CRM do you find most attractive? Why?
4. What kind of employment in CRM do you find least attractive? Why?

Notes

1. See Title 36, Part 800 of the Code of Federal Regulations (36 CFR Part 800) at https://www.achp.gov/sites/default/files/regulations/2017-02/regs-rev04.pdf.
2. https://therevelator.org/rivers-legal-rights/.
3. There are fine distinctions between social and cultural anthropology, and not all university anthropology departments reflect all the fields. There are also lots of sub-subfields like economic anthropology, medical anthropology, underwater archaeology, human evolution, and forensic biological anthropology.
4. https://en.wikipedia.org/wiki/Regulatory_agency.
5. Cf. https://www.law.cornell.edu/cfr/text/33/320.4.
6. https://www.fws.gov/midwest/endangered/permits/hcp/hcp_wofactsheet.html.
7. https://www.epa.gov/environmentaljustice/environmental-justice-2020-action -agenda.
8. See 40 CFR 1508.16(g) at https://www.law.cornell.edu/cfr/text/40/1502.16.
9. Spoiler alert: it's the political leadership.
10. https://www.lrl.usace.army.mil/Portals/64/docs/regulatory/Coordination/33%20 CFR%20325%20Appendix%20C.pdf.
11. There's a good deal of "gray" literature on this subject. For some of my own ruminations on this topic, see my blog at http://crmplus.blogspot.com/2011/12/corps-of-engineers-needs-appendectomy.html.

Further Reading

What Is CRM and Where Did It Come From?

Advisory Council on Historic Preservation (United States). n.d. *National Historic Preservation Act of 1966, As Amended through 1992.* https://www.nps.gov/history/local-law/nhpa1966.htm.
> The NHPA is the primary law guiding CRM in the United States. The other is the National Environmental Policy Act (NEPA); see https://www.energy.gov/nepa/downloads/national-environmental-policy-act-1969.

Connally, Ernest Allen. 1986. "Origins of the National Historic Preservation Act 1966."
    CRM Bulletin 9(1): 7–10. A publication of the United States National Park Service.
    https://www.nps.gov/CRMJournal/CRMBulletin/v9n1.pdf.
        Connally, an architectural historian, was one of the architects of the United
    States National Historic Preservation Act and the National Park Service pro-
    grams to implement it. He also had considerable influence on international
    practice.

Giacinto, Adam. 2011. "A Qualitative History of 'Cultural Resource' Management."
    Anthropologies, 15 May. http://www.anthropologiesproject.org/2011/05/qualitative-
    history-of-cultural.html.
        A thoughtful postmodern archaeological perspective on CRM.

Harrison, Rodney. 2012. *Heritage: Critical Approaches*. New York: Routledge.
        An international perspective on heritage/CRM.

King, Thomas F. (1998) 2012. *Cultural Resource Laws and Practice*. 4th ed. Lanham, MD:
    Altamira Press.
        My effort to make sense of United States CRM in general.

Lipe, William D., and Alexander J. Lindsay, eds. 1974. *Proceedings of the 1974 Cultural
    Resource Management Conference, Federal Center, Denver, Colorado*. Museum of
    Northern Arizona Technical Series No. 14. Flagstaff: Northern Arizona Society of
    Science and Art.
        The publication in which (to my knowledge) the term "cultural resource man-
    agement" first appeared.

McGimsey, Charles R., III, and Hester A. Davis, eds. 1977. *The Management of Archeo-
    logical Resources: The Airlie House Report*. Washington, DC: Society for American
    Archaeology.
        The results of an early conference designed to plot the future of archaeological
    CRM in the United States.

National Preservation Institute. n.d. "What Are 'Cultural Resources'?" https://www.
    npi.org/what-are-cultural-resources.
        NPI is a major provider of training in United States CRM.

Peebles, Giovanna M. 2013. "Looking Back at Archaeology and Cultural Resources
    Management in the United States and Vermont Through a Forty-Year Mirror." *Jour-
    nal of Vermont Archaeology* 13: 19–62. A publication of the Vermont Archaeological
    Society, ed. Niels R. Rinehart. http://www.vtarchaeology.org/wp-content/uploads/
    v13_ch2_reduced.pdf.
        A comprehensive review of United States CRM from the standpoint of a State
    Historic Preservation Officer who happens to be an archaeologist.

Wikipedia. n.d. "Cultural Resources Management." https://en.wikipedia.org/wiki/
    Cultural_resources_management.
        As of September 2019, a pretty good definition and description of CRM. See
    also Wikipedia, "Cultural Heritage Management," https://en.wikipedia.org/
    wiki/Cultural_heritage_management.

What CRM Is Supposed to Accomplish

Journal of Cultural Heritage Management and Sustainable Development. http://www. emeraldgrouppublishing.com/products/journals/journals.htm?id=jchmsd.
Articles in this journal provide a broad summary of what CRM is and does in various parts of the world.

King, Thomas F., ed. 2011. *A Companion to Cultural Resource Management.* London: Wiley-Blackwell.
Me again, and this one is way too expensive to buy; check it in your library. Its chapters, by a wide variety of specialists in different kinds and aspects of CRM, give an overview of what the field collectively tries to do.

National Park Service. n.d. "What Is Historic Preservation?" https://www.nps.gov/ subjects/historicpreservation/what-is-historic-preservation.htm.
A good summary of the historic preservation part of CRM from the United States National Park Service's point of view.

Smith, Laurajane. 2006. *Uses of Heritage.* New York: Routledge.
Smith's postmodern take on what heritage (aka "cultural resources") may be good for.

Who Does CRM?

Cauvin, Thomas. 2016. *Public History: A Textbook of Practice.* New York: Routledge.
As its title indicates, a textbook of practice in public history, an important element of CRM.

Cragoe, Carol Davidson. 2008. *How to Read Buildings: A Crash Course in Architectural Styles.* New York: Rizzoli.
An overview of architectural history from an American perspective.

Hutchings, Rich, and Marina La Salle. 2015. "Archaeology as Disaster Capitalism." *International Journal of Historical Archaeology* 19(4): 699–720. https://link.springer. com/article/10.1007/s10761-015-0308-3.
A critical postmodern take on archaeology, notably as practiced in CRM.

King, Thomas F. (2005) 2016. *Doing Archaeology: A Cultural Resource Management Perspective.* New York: Routledge.
My attempt to discuss archaeology as a part of CRM.

Mercier, Laurie, and Madeline Buckendorf. 2010. *Using Oral History in Community History Projects.* Murfreesboro, TN: Oral History Association.
Oral history, like documentary history, is an important part of CRM.

Tyler, Norman, Ted J. Ligibel, and Ilene R. Tyler. (1994) 2009. *Historic Preservation: An Introduction to Its History, Principles, and Practice.* 2nd ed. New York: Norton.
The historic preservation face of CRM as understood by its most strictly architectural practitioners, primarily focused on working in local government.

Communities in CRM

Convention on Biological Diversity, Secretariat of. 2004. *Akwé: Kon Guidelines.* Montreal. https://www.cbd.int/doc/publications/akwe-brochure-en.pdf.
>   Commonsense guidelines from the international biological profession about how to address the cultural interests and values of indigenous and local communities.

James Kent Associates and International Right of Way Association. 2016. "Social Ecology: A Special Collection of Articles on the Art and Science of Social Ecology." *Right of Way Magazine: An Anthology.* http://jkagroup.com/Docs/IRWA-20170203-Anthology.pdf.
>   Kent and his colleagues come at communities in CRM (without mentioning the term) from a mostly sociological perspective.

Parker, Patricia, and Thomas F. King. 1990. *Guidelines for Identifying and Documenting Traditional Cultural Properties.* National Register Bulletin 38. Washington DC, United States National Park Service. https://www.nps.gov/nr/publications/bulletins/nrb38/.
>   Stresses the need to involve communities in the identification of historic places, and to accept the significance of such places as understood by communities.

Rio Tinto. 2016. *Why Cultural Heritage Matters: A Resource Guide for Integrating Cultural Heritage Management into Communities Work at Rio Tinto.* http://www.riotinto.com/documents/ReportsPublications/Rio_Tinto_Cultural_Heritage_Guide.pdf.
>   This guide, put out by a well-known international mineral extraction company, helps explain why CRM is good business.

Clients

American Cultural Resources Association (ACRA). n.d. http://www.acra-crm.org/.
>   This organization is made up of CRM firms, whose major preoccupation is with providing service to clients.

Heritage Business Journal. https://heritagebusinessjournal.com/tag/cultural-resource-management/.
>   This journal deals with the business of CRM, which is very much about client relations.

Regulators

Advisory Council on Historic Preservation (United States). n.d. http://www.achp.gov/.
>   The ACHP oversees compliance with Section 106 of the United States National Historic Preservation Act (NHPA). Its regulations dictate how project review under Section 106 is to be carried out.

National Association of Tribal Historic Preservation Officers (United States). n.d. http://www.nathpo.org.
>   THPOs carry out essentially the same functions as SHPOs within the boundaries of Indian reservations in the United States.

National Conference of State Historic Preservation Officers (United States). n.d. http://www.ncshpo.org.

> The SHPOs are the regulators with whom CRM practitioners in the United States will most often come into contact, and for whom some CRM practitioners work.

Working Directly for the Government

Go Government. n.d. http://www.gogovernment.org/government_101/pros_and_cons _of_working_in_government.php.

> This website, maintained by the Partnership for Public Service, provides a pretty balanced view of working for the United States government.

Rush, Laurie, and Russell Kaldenberg. 2006. *Cultural Resources in the Department of Defense: Planning for the Future.* https://www.denix.osd.mil/cr/cultural-resources-program-management/archaeology/uploads/current-dod-needs-for-crm-archaeology-laurie-rush-fort-drum-ny-and-russell-kaldenberg-naws-china-lake-ca/.

> This slide show illustrates some of the concerns of CRM specialists working for the United States Department of Defense. Kaldenberg also has a chapter about working for the government in my 2011 reader, *Companion to Cultural Resource Management*, referenced above.

Chapter 2

What CRM Archaeologists Do
Consultation and Identification

So if you get a job in CRM, how will you spend your time? What will you do? CRM carries with it a high degree of unpredictability, but let's try to break it down. In this chapter we'll look at some of the things we *always* do; in subsequent chapters we'll examine things that are a little less commonplace.

We Consult/Negotiate

It's probably not what you'll get assigned to do right off the bat, but consultation is a big, big part of CRM, and you'll need to do a lot of it as you move up the ladder in your organization, firm, or agency. You'll consult with clients; you'll consult with project proponents; you'll consult with regulators. And I *hope*, though it's often sadly ignored, you'll consult with the people out there on the ground who care about the "cultural resources" that a project may muck up, and about other things that are *not* obviously cultural resources, such as property rights, tax rates, the cost of electricity, the non-cultural environment.

The NEPA and NHPA regulations assign *formal* consulting responsibilities to the government agencies that comply with the laws, and particularly where Indian tribes are involved, this responsibility may be quite jealously guarded. "Government-to-government" consultation—effectively required by the treaty relationships between the United States government and tribes—obviously must be carried out by governments, *not* by consulting firms or project proponents. But consultation, even between governments, is carried out by human beings, and the humans who are formally tasked with consulting—if they're smart—will turn to experts for assistance. So while you and your employer may not personally be the ones consulting with tribes, local governments, and others, you'll probably be involved in consultation in at least some kind of advisory role. And CRM involves a lot of less formal consultation, in which everyone gets involved.

Merriam-Webster Online tells us that "consult" can simply mean to "consider" or "to ask the advice or opinion" of someone. Rather more helpfully, it says consultation can mean "to deliberate together." *Deliberate*. Ponder an issue together. Seek mutually understood conclusions. All of these involve communicating with people. *With* them, not just *to* them. That's an important distinction. Back and forth, give and take, hear/read what others have to say, speak/write to be understood. Most of us are not very good at this sort of communication, and it's worth at least thinking about it, or preferably getting some specialized training.

Deliberating together also almost always means trying to *negotiate agreement—reaching a meeting of the minds about what to do.* This leads to getting agreements committed to writing, and making sure that what's written actually captures what's been agreed to. Whatever's written down ought to be easy to understand and follow. Truly good-faith deliberation includes trying to make sure that any terms agreed to are in fact followed. These are super-important aspects of consultation that are far too often forgotten or ignored.

With whom do you consult? Well, your employer, your client, regulators, and experts in other fields like engineering, biology, and hydrology, but also— critically—with the people who may be affected by whatever your agency or client is considering doing. This may be tricky, because the potentially affected people may not speak your language—sometimes literally. You speak English or Chinese, they speak Spanish or Swahili. Or it may be a matter of vernaculars. You may use academic jargon that makes you seem uppity, cutting off conversation. They may use local slang and assume you understand local events, personalities, and histories about which you haven't a clue. Or you just may talk past one another.

There are lots of books on aspects of consultation and negotiation, and training can be obtained from a variety of sources. Several of these are listed under "Further Reading" at the end of this chapter. Most directly relevant to most CRM practitioners in the United States are the NHPA Section 106 regulations of the ACHP, and related guidelines issued by the NPS.

The Section 106 regulations, at 36 CFR 800.16(f), define "consultation" as "the process of seeking, discussing, and considering the views of other participants, and, where feasible, seeking agreement with them regarding matters arising in the section 106 process."[1] They go on to refer to the NPS's "Standards and Guidelines for Federal Agency Historic Preservation Programs Pursuant to the National Historic Preservation Act" for further guidance. Among much else (the "Standards and Guidelines" are pretty wordy), these say that "whether consulting on a specific project, or on broader agency programs, the agency should:

- make its interests and constraints clear at the beginning;
- make clear any rules, processes, or schedules applicable to the consultation;
- acknowledge others' interests as legitimate, and seek to understand them;

• develop and consider a full range of options; and,
• try to identify solutions that will leave all parties satisfied."[2]

They note that "although time limits may be necessary on specific transactions carried out in the course of consultation (e.g., the time allowed to respond to an inquiry), there should be no hard-and-fast time limit on consultation overall. Consultation on a specific undertaking should proceed until agreement is reached or until it becomes clear to the agency that agreement cannot be reached."

The "Standards and Guidelines" are intended to promote *respectful* consultation with those whose cultural heritage, ways of life, and livelihoods may be changed by your agency's or client's actions. This doesn't mean that you have to pander; it just means that you ought to treat those with whom you're consulting as responsible, thoughtful adults—even when they don't behave that way. Listen to what they say; pay attention. Hear them out. Ask questions if you don't understand. Treat them as human beings, and acknowledge your own humanity, your own limitations.

Throughout any CRM-related process under United States federal law—and I'd recommend it even where such law doesn't apply—you and your employer and your client need to be prepared to consult with potentially affected people by "acknowledg[ing] others' interests" as legitimate and trying to identify solutions "that will leave all parties satisfied." And you need to be prepared to take the necessary time either to reach an agreement or to conclude that an agreement can't be reached and document why.

But—and it's a big but—your client, or your company's client, may not *want* you to consult with anyone, or at least not with anyone other than people they approve. This usually means people on their payroll or otherwise on their list of "friendlies." There are some legitimate reasons for this sort of secrecy, like avoiding the release of trade secrets or not driving up the price of real estate that the client wants to acquire, as well as uncertainties about who has the responsibility and authority to consult. But whether there's a good reason for it or not, failure to consult is a serious problem. Cultural resources wouldn't be "cultural" if they weren't somehow valued by people, and it's awfully hard— even impossible—to figure out why something is important, or even what it is, or what to do about it, without talking to the people who may value it. Yes, you can probably say, on the basis of your own knowledge, that from *an archaeological standpoint* a stratified site with lots of ancient architecture and artifacts is pretty important and that a scatter of potsherds in a plowed field maybe isn't. But from the standpoint of the people descended from whoever dropped those potsherds, it may be another matter entirely. And those people may also ascribe importance to the willow grove or waterfall or rock outcrop that has no evident archaeological value at all. And the old woman who's been collecting artifacts in the area all her life may be able to tell you that the place where those sherds are scattered is really an old burial place, because she's seen bones plowed up there. All these are things that you need to understand, and you can't do it without talking to people. Your clients, if they're smart, know that they need to understand such things, so the burial place or waterfall doesn't rise up as a last-minute, unexpected challenge to their plans.

I'm sorry to observe that a lot of CRM practitioners just accept the demands of clients that they not talk to people. It's an understandable business decision, but it really tears the guts out of CRM. If your clients demand secrecy, I strongly suggest that you try to explain that you can't really do the job without talking to people, and that consultation with interested parties is required by the Section 106 regulations (if they apply), and then see what you can negotiate.

The fact that you *can't* do the job without talking to people may be a surprise to your clients, because many have bought into the notion that CRM experts are able to figure out what's "culturally important" based solely on their own expertise. After all, a biologist or hydrologist or traffic expert can do that. And some CRM practitioners, sadly, have similarly inflated views of themselves.

Exactly what you—or your supervisors—can do about this problem is hard to say, because the client may indeed have good reasons for keeping things quiet. And, of course, because he or she can fire you. But failing to consult people is a really good formula for doing bad CRM and for last-minute disasters, so if your clients call on you to avoid talking to people, I recommend that you try to get them to rethink their position.

If you're working directly for a government agency, there should be little excuse for secrecy; after all, the government works for the people, doesn't it? But government people can be just as averse to consultation as private clients can. It's troublesome to talk with people: it takes time, and the people often don't speak a bureaucrat's language. And for military and intelligence agencies, "national defense" exceptions to consultation requirements can be interpreted pretty expansively. For all our rhetoric in the United States about government being of, by, and for the people, our laws don't provide very well for involving "the people" in government operations. The NEPA regulations, for example, treat "the public" pretty much as a passive recipient of information compiled by experts, and demand consultation only with other experts and people in authority. The NHPA regulations, and indeed the law itself since 1992, are a good deal more directive about consultation, but they are not always attended to.

I've found, though, that usually people in authority—clients and agency people—can be made to understand that consulting affected people is a good idea. It helps to avoid surprises, to build partnerships, and, if nothing else, to comply meaningfully with the law.[3]

Of course, you need to document the processes and fruits of consultation. Whom did you talk with? What did you talk about? Who said what? What if anything was agreed to? What follow-up needs to be done? How will it be done? So keep good notes; consider maintaining a diary or logbook. Make photographic, video, and audio records, being careful to get and document the permission of people you record and to clarify any ownership issues. Be careful about discarding drafts. Digitize project paperwork before recycling it.

And again, understand that the responsibility to consult formally with Indian tribes and others under United States law is vested only in federal agencies. But consultation needs to be *informed*, and you and your employer are likely to be the ones to gather and try to make sense of the information that makes consultation possible. That gathering and sense making itself requires consultation—whether or not it's understood to be the sort of formal consultation to which the regulations refer. Whatever government officials may say, in CRM we're consulting all the time; it's fundamental to our work.

We Try to Identify "Cultural Resources"

When you get your first job in CRM, you'll probably be on a team tasked with identifying "cultural resources." It's generally understood that you can't manage cultural resources without identifying them first. Actually, that's a pretty gross oversimplification, despite the fact that almost everybody tosses it off as a truism. For instance, we don't have to swim down and find all the shipwrecks in a harbor to know that dredging the harbor will almost certainly muck up a bunch of shipwrecks—assuming we have *some* evidence that ships have sunk there. We don't have to plot every artifact on the ground along a pipeline right-of-way to know that putting in the pipeline will undoubtedly churn up some archaeological sites.

Still, at some point you're going to have to look for the "cultural resources" that your client's project may muck up, or that your agency is responsible for managing. If you're trying to assess the effects of a proposed project, the earlier you can do this, the better. Most CRM practitioners spend most of their time (when not reviewing reports and project plans) engaged in some sort of resource identification.

So what are you looking to identify? You may say "archaeological sites, stupid," but you need to remember those "cultural resources" that *aren't* archaeological sites. These include old buildings and structures, of course, and places linked to a community's traditions—the waterfall, the willow grove, the rock outcrop—even if there's nothing there for archaeologists to examine.

Pop quiz: would you regard such things as "tangible" cultural resources, or are they "intangible"?

Tangible/Intangible

An archaeological site is obviously a *tangible* thing, a physical thing. You can walk on it, dig a hole in it. Likewise with a building: you can grab its doorknob, open the door, and walk in. Most of CRM involves finding, evaluating, and managing such tangible things.

But what makes an archaeological site worth noticing, thinking about? Most archaeologists would say it's the information the site contains. That information is *intangible*—made up of complex interactions between the physical stuff in the ground and the operations of our minds. To an architectural historian, a building is important for what it illustrates about some aspect of architecture as practiced in the past—a style, a way of building things, a kind of decoration. These too are intangible, of the mind. The family that's lived in the house for seven generations, or the indigenous community whose ancestors lived at the site, probably ascribes values to it that can variously be called "spiritual" or "sentimental" or "loving." These are intangible too, but really no more intangible than an archaeologist's hypothesis, a pottery typology, or an architectural style. *We can't responsibly evaluate or manage a tangible cultural resource without respecting and addressing its intangible values.*

There are some cultural resources that are more or less *entirely* intangible. In 2004, UNESCO member nations agreed on treaty titled "Convention for the Safeguarding of the Intangible Cultural Heritage." "Cultural heritage," remember, means the same thing as "cultural resource." The Convention's website gives an idea of what UNESCO members think intangible cultural heritage/resources are.[4] Examples include women's chants in Nigeria, a traditional dance form in Armenia, *punto* music in Cuba, and the festival of the Sacred Pitcher in India. Song, dance, celebration—but this doesn't exhaust the list. Traditions of food procurement and preparation, forms of recreation, and a wide array of artistic practices have also been identified as intangible cultural heritage. Then there's language itself. Language loss has been identified as an extremely serious problem worldwide, "with great humanistic and scientific consequences,"[5] and traditional languages are under continual assault by the forces of modernity.

In identifying cultural resources, we obviously ought to look for both those that are tangible (recognizing their intangible qualities) and those that are entirely intangible. In practice, sadly, intangible heritage tends to get short shrift—precisely because it *is* intangible. Bookshelves groan with the weight of literature on how to recognize, evaluate, document, and manage buildings, sites, artifacts, art, and other kinds of tangible heritage, but intangibilities are quite a different matter. There's plenty of handwringing about the loss of languages, stories, songs, spiritual beliefs, folkways, and traditional ecological knowledge, but very little practical guidance on what to do about it. It remains a fact that intangible heritage is a critical part of the cultural environment—in some ways the *most* critical. Failing to recognize this can greatly complicate your client's project or your agency's operations. You need to try to understand what intangible cultural resources are and think about ways to manage them, but the laws and regulations don't give you much guidance. It's a challenging area of practice, to which most of us, myself included, haven't given enough attention. If you're up for a challenge, this is one—or a bundle—to take up.

Identification Steps

Generally speaking, the identification of "cultural resources" involves several more or less sequential (but often overlapping) steps.

APE definition. "APE" is a term of art invented under Section 106 of the NHPA. It means "area(s) of potential effects," that is, the area or areas where whatever it is that's proposed (highway, apartment building, reservoir) has the potential to affect historic properties, whether such properties are known to be there or not.

Effects are generally understood to fall into three overlapping categories:

1. Direct effects: Where a project will knock down, root out, dig up, or otherwise disturb something as a direct result of its implementation—right here, right now;
2. Indirect effects: Where something is likely to be knocked down, rooted out, dug up, or otherwise disturbed sometime in the future, or off someplace in the distance, but arguably because the project has been implemented;
3. Cumulative effects: Where things are getting disturbed, or otherwise changed somehow, over time by multiple causes, and the project will contribute somehow to this pattern of change.

All kinds of effects are supposed to be considered under the NEPA, the NHPA, and similar laws, so all should be involved in defining the APE.

Some agencies make much of the fact that APE definition is a government responsibility, and tell consultants and others to just shut up and work within the APEs that the agencies define. There are good reasons for this—the agencies are in theory more objective than, say, project proponents and their consultants. But on the other hand, those who define the APE need to be informed, and often need help thinking through the issues involved. There, if nowhere else, is where you and your employer may come in.

I dreamed up the term and acronym APE in the mid-1980s while working on the Section 106 regulations, and I regret having done so; I think it's created more trouble than it's worth. It tempts people to split hairs—is this location or that in or out of the APE? But it's a concept that's hard to avoid. You've got to figure out where to consider potential effects, and the place to look is obviously the place(s) where you think that effects may occur. If you're looking at putting in a reservoir on the South Fork of the Wandering River, you're probably going to want to look mostly along the South Fork—not on top of Pointypeak Mountain 700 kilometers away. Unless, of course, the project includes something like a power line that will extend over the top of the mountain, or the project will screw up the view from the mountaintop.

So you look at your project plans and ask yourself and others, including people the project may affect, "where might this project have effects on cultural resources?" Of course, under Section 106 you're required to consider only effects on tangible "historic properties," but it's wise to think broadly, because even if people are mostly concerned about effects on some utterly intangible thing, there are probably ways to link it to historic properties. Places that figure importantly in the local language, for instance, or places whose smells are culturally valued, may be eligible for the NRHP or otherwise important to consider in impact assessment.[6] Draw lines on the map to embrace all such areas, and that's your APE, at least for now. It may shrink or grow or shape-change as you learn more about it, and that's OK.

Don't worry about whether you have access to the APE—whether you'll be able to do an archaeological survey there, or whatever. You may not need to do an archaeological survey, and if you do need to do one, it may or may not be necessary to get access to the land. These are issues to be addressed later.

Background research. This involves reviewing what's known about an area's environment, its geomorphology, its people and communities living and dead, its history and prehistory and architecture, its place-names and maybe its smells, all aimed at figuring out what's likely to be in the APE that needs managing. This step may include undertaking remote sensing studies—examining aerial photos, sidescan sonar, Lidar imaging, satellite imagery, and the like—to find things that, while tangible, aren't obvious on the ground, or that are in inaccessible or hazardous locations. Doing background research is also an important way to find out about intangible heritage—the fact, say, that everybody really likes the view from Nibbly Knob, or that the annual catfish catching contest is carried out in the Roiling Rapids.

Background research ought to involve identifying the people with whom you'll need to consult, figuring out how best to consult them, and encouraging them to consult. Fred McGhee, a collaborator on this book, reminds me that best practices often overlap with those of community organizing—finding out who the community's leaders are, engaging them in dialogue, helping them understand the issues and frame their concerns.[7] This may seem pretty aggressive to your client, but if you don't know that there are people who care about the APE's cultural resources, you're not likely to consult them about their concerns—until they take your client or agency to court, or until your project has screwed over whatever aspects of the APE concerned them.

Sadly, in a lot of cases background research gets reduced to doing a "records check" to see what's listed in available "inventories" like the World Heritage List, the NRHP or its equivalent, or an SHPO's files. This results in finding only what's been formally recorded. There are times when such "inventories" are relatively comprehensive and complete, but most times they're not; there are almost always things out there in the environment that have not been documented. And of course, what has been recorded will inevitably be only those kinds of things that people thought of as "cultural resources" (or whatever) at the time the inventory was compiled; plus, the inventory will reflect the biases and assumptions of its compilers. It may be biased toward fine old buildings or toward archaeological sites of a particular kind. It's rare for an inventory to say much about cultural landscapes or culturally important trees, let alone intangible heritage. And of course, it does nothing to identify the living people who ought to be consulted about impacts on any of these things.

So if you possibly can, you should go beyond "records checks" and undertake real, thoughtful background research. Exactly what this entails will depend on the area's environment, history, and culture. Background research should not only tell you what's already been recorded about an area's cultural resources (however defined); it should also give you a basis for *predicting* what's out there that *hasn't* yet been recorded.

Background research should also help you figure out what fieldwork methods will be needed. Are there likely to be deeply buried prehistoric sites, demanding test excavation or the deployment of ground penetrating radar? Are there likely to be graves or scattered human remains that could be identified by forensic canines? Is there a local community whose members speak an uncommon language, suggesting the need for interpreters? Does the community have preferred ways of communicating with outsiders, or with government officials? Are there likely to be culturally important plants that can be identified only by trained ethnobotanists and/or traditional experts?

Scoping. Answers to questions like those above, the results of background research in general, need to be organized into a "scope of work" or work plan for identification. That plan should be based not only on your background research but also on consultation with others, including experts, regulators, community leaders, and interested or affected members of the public. Developing such a plan is often referred to as "scoping."

In my experience, scoping is one of the most important—and neglected— parts of CRM. Good, early scoping will maximize the likelihood that you'll find everything that needs to be found, recognize everything that needs to be recognized, and give everything its proper weight and value. But scoping is often treated as a pro forma exercise: "We will have our scoping meeting and record the results and ignore them." That's sad, dumb, and counterproductive. Scoping ought to take the results of background research, expose them to expert and public scrutiny, revise them as needed, and translate them into a scope of work that someone—like you—can carry out.

But if you're just getting started, as the low person on the totem pole, chances are you'll just be handed the scope of work and told to execute it. Or worse yet, you'll be told to go out and identify "cultural resources" (or something) following some standard protocol developed by the SHPO or its equivalent, or by the local archaeological community. Or worst of all (though it may give you opportunities to be creative), as the new staff archaeologist you may just be expected to *know* what to do, *without* an explicit scope of work. If so, good luck. I'd still strongly recommend doing background research and developing a work plan—even if no one sees it but you. Ideally, though, you'll share your plan with others and consult them to improve it before you go out in the field and start implementing it.

Examining the APE. Equipped with the results of background research, and with luck a scope of work based on that research, you head for "the field" to look for stuff. "The field" may be a 1,000-kilometer pipeline corridor, an urban neighborhood, a river valley, a mountain. Generally, it's all or parts of an APE—remember, that's a proposed project's area of "potential effects." In other words, it's the area or areas where the project has the potential to affect stuff—directly, indirectly, or as part of a pattern of "cumulative effect."

The APE may have multiple parts, in each of which particular identification methods may be appropriate. There may be a visual APE, from which project elements like roads or towers will be visible. There may be an auditory APE, where the operation of facilities like pumping plants and quarries will be audible. An olfactory APE may embrace the areas where the smell of a project, such as an asphalt plant or a rubber-processing facility, may be noticeable. There's almost always a physical APE made up of areas where the project will disturb land or vegetation or buildings.

Your identification work may extend *beyond* the areas where specific auditory, visual, olfactory, and physical effects may occur. For example, if a project may affect traditional fishing practices, that's a cultural resource issue that needs to be considered even if there's no specific location where the project will mess with the practices. If it may alter water quality, and if water quality is culturally important, then that's an issue that needs to be addressed. If the landscape in which the project would be built is one to which a group ascribes spiritual or other cultural importance, then the whole landscape has to be characterized somehow so that impacts on it can be considered.

The kind of identification you do in each of these sub-APEs is specific to the kinds of impacts that are expected. There may be no reason whatever to do archaeological survey in the auditory or olfactory APE. There may be little reason for archaeological survey in the visual APE. But auditory and visual and olfactory effects—to say nothing of spiritual effects—may be of great concern to the people who will experience them, so an important part of identification is finding those people and asking what they think the effects will be.

The chances are that none of this will be explained to you, and you'll simply be directed to go out and do an archaeological survey of the direct physical APE—that is, the area or areas where the project will physically disturb the ground or knock down buildings. If that's what happens, that's what happens, but you need to know, and your supervisors ought to know, that *the laws aren't just about physical impacts on things like archaeological sites.* The NEPA and the NHPA require that all kinds of impacts be considered on all kinds of cultural (and under NEPA, other) resources, or in the case of the NHPA on all kinds of historic properties. Your supervisors or your clients may choose to ignore these requirements, but they may get in trouble as a result. *You* shouldn't get in trouble if you're simply doing what you're told, but there's no guarantee. And your reputation is likely to suffer.

So what kind of fieldwork do you do? That depends on what your background research has told you. Ignoring my frets about CRM not being about archaeology, let's start with archaeology, because it's easy for archaeologists to grasp.

Archaeological survey. Maybe your background research has told you that there may be deeply buried prehistoric sites in some part of the APE. In that case, if your project is likely to disturb them—that is, if it involves deep excavation for a pipeline or basements or wells or whatever—you need to plan for deep testing of some kind, probably using augers, backhoes, and/or remote-sensing. Maybe you've learned that there were ancient earthworks that have now been flattened; in this case you may need to use remote-sensing technology like airborne Lidar to tease out their remnant traces. Or maybe during your background research you talked with local artifact collectors who told you that the very best time to find artifacts is in the autumn after the grass turns brown, but you need to do your survey in the spring. You're going to have to figure out some way to accommodate these visibility issues—maybe by plowing the area and then walking over it carefully, looking at the ground.

If your background research has given you reason to think that there is something special at a particular location—for example, if an archaeological site is reported to be at a particular place in the landscape—then you'll want to check it out. You'll typically walk or drive to it, and then walk all over it, looking at its surface, checking to see what burrowing rodents or insects might be bringing up, and maybe digging some test holes. If your background research has suggested that a type of landform is likely to contain something—such as fishing camps around the margins of a lake—then you're going to want to give similar attention to such areas. Think about—and, importantly, talk with knowledgeable people about—how fishing camps are likely to be expressed in and on the ground in such an area. But don't ignore places and landforms where nothing is reported or suspected.

If members of the cultural group associated with the area—for example, an indigenous group's elders or longtime farmers and ranchers—are willing to help you, you ought to go into the field with them and listen carefully to what they have to say about what they see there. They may not tell you that there is an archaeological site at a particular location, but they may say that a family or person used to live at that location, or that something used to be done there, or that something happened there according to their traditions. This is all very important information that not only can lead you to identifying important cultural resources (tangible and intangible) but also can allow you to interpret them and understand what makes them important.

If all else fails, and, for example, you just have to survey a ten-mile right-of-way 50 meters wide through cow pastures and farm fields, then commonly what's done is to walk "transects," that is, to spread people out at set distances like 5 or 10 meters apart and have them walk on a set compass heading, looking carefully at the ground, examining any exposures of the soil where rodents or insects have brought subsurface material to the surface, and scraping suspicious locations with trowels to see if anything turns up. The idea is to be able to say, at the end of the day, that you carefully inspected the entire area and either found things or concluded on some rational basis that there wasn't anything there to be found.

Where the surface is obscured or stuff is likely to be buried, it's common practice to carry out some kind of test excavation. Typically, each team member will walk a certain number of paces in a particular direction and then dig a hole. Maybe it'll be a round hole, or a square hole, usually of particular dimensions and dug to a particular depth. I don't know of anyone who digs triangular holes, but it's not unimaginable. You'll fill out some kind of record on each hole, typically recording its location, its dimensions and shape, its depth, and its stratigraphy. Sometimes you'll record the color of the soil in each stratum, usually with reference to a Munsell soil color chart,[8] and sometimes you'll record its texture using a standard system.[9] Of course, you'll record any artifacts or other evidence of cultural activity that you find—for example, fire-cracked rocks, flakes of stone, or burned earth. You may or may not retain artifacts or other items for later analysis. Doing so depends on the overall field-work plan and is influenced by factors such as land ownership, local laws and regulations, local sensitivities, and cost considerations.

The size, shape, and spacing of test holes—often called shovel test pits, or shovel test units, or test units, and referred to colloquially by their acronyms (STP, STU, etc.)—are often subjects of vigorous debate in regional CRM circles. Or they're dictated by the government or some authoritative archaeological body, and everybody adheres to them.

If you're someplace where archaeological sites are likely to be deeply buried, you'll have to adapt. In China, for example, archaeologists routinely use the "Chinese auger," a hand-driven or powered tool that can pull cores of sediment from several meters below the surface.

Non-archaeological survey. Meanwhile, someone—you or someone else on your team—needs to be looking into non-archaeological or extra-archaeological cultural resources that may be subject not only to physical effect but also to visual, auditory, olfactory, or other effect. That, of course, requires consulting the people who may see, hear, smell, or otherwise experience the effects of the project.

This is a lot less cut and dried than is archaeological survey. It involves finding people, engaging them in conversation, and trying to understand their concerns. They may tell you things that help you interpret your archaeological survey data. For example, people who have lived on the land for a long time may be able to tell you about things that were found there in the past, perhaps at different seasons or after floods or fires that removed vegetation or where buildings now obscure the surface. And of course, members of a group whose ancestors lived on the land generations ago may be able to explain things that you see on or in the ground that would be quite inexplicable to you without their help. Or they may tell you about places that aren't archaeological at all, but that are culturally important to them—the place where wild onions can be gathered, or the place where Earthwalker fought with the Great Lizard.

Rock art. Archaeologists tend to look at the ground, which is right and proper, but you need to remember that there are important things above the ground as well. In many parts of the world, rock art (petroglyphs, pictographs, geoglyphs) is an important kind of cultural resource.[10] Identifying rock art requires special tools, special techniques, and special bodies of expertise, so these will need to be arranged for if rock art's likely to be present.

Vegetation and animals. Trees and other plants may be culturally important to a concerned community, as may the animals that live among them. This might mean the need to consult specialists—not only the botanists, biologists, and ecologists retained by your firm or agency to characterize and evaluate things animal and vegetal, but also expert ethnobiologists and especially people with traditional knowledge of local plants and animals. Traditional ecological knowledge (with the catchy acronym TEK)[11] is getting increasing attention among natural resource specialists, so you may find that the notion of attending to it will not be entirely foreign to your biological and ecological colleagues.

Architecture and engineering. And then of course there are structures and buildings. These tend to be regarded by government cultural resource authorities as the province of architectural and engineering historians, and of course they are, so you need to have access to people with these kinds of expertise. But they also may have other kinds of cultural significance. People lived in them (and may still), operated them, worked in them, worshiped in them, went to school in them, or were imprisoned or executed in them. Finding out about these kinds of significance may be a job for a historian or cultural anthropologist—or for an archaeologist sensitive to these aspects of significance.

Intangibles. Identifying intangible cultural resources is pretty much going to depend on background research and consultation. Is there something in the local history books indicating that something special takes place in the area? A religious observance? A sporting event? Mushroom gathering? What does the local librarian have to say? The Chamber of Commerce? If your work is being done under something like the NEPA or NHPA, there should be some kind of scoping during which members of the public have the opportunity to take part; this may provide opportunities to collect information. The main things to do are to ask questions and listen to answers. And of course, record what you observe, hear, or otherwise learn—unless people insist on speaking off the record; you have to respect such requests.

Reporting. Fieldwork will lead to the preparation of some kind of report. Exactly what kind of report depends on what's required by clients and regulators. Typically, though, the report will describe the area inspected, the people involved in inspecting it, the dates the work was done, the methods employed, any problems encountered, the results of the work, and any uncertainties that ought to be taken into account in interpreting the results. If anything was found, then the report will probably offer recommendations as to its character and significance.

In the United States, rather confusingly because they don't do the kinds of surveys required by most CRM operations, there is a trio of official government historic property "survey" programs. These are descended from one set up during the Great Depression of the 1930s as an emergency employment program, administered by the National Park Service. The Historic American Buildings Survey (HABS) and its offshoots, the Historic American Engineering Record (HAER) and the Historic American Landscapes Survey (HALS)— support detailed documentation of historic buildings, engineering works, and landscapes; their records are filed with the Library of Congress. HABS/HAER/HALS operate pretty much in their own world, but you should know they exist.

Study Questions

1. Does the prospect of consulting/negotiating with diverse interest groups bother you? Why or why not? If it does bother you, what can you do to overcome it?
2. Find a project that's proposed in your area or elsewhere. Google "Construction projects in (state, province, or region)" if you're hard up for ideas. What do you think the APE(s) of this project should be? Why?
3. Given this APE or these APEs, can you imagine what a scope of work for identification might look like? Please draft an outline.
4. In doing background research for a project in an area that interests you, what sources do you think you'd need to consult? What challenges might there be in doing so?
5. What might be involved in doing fieldwork on a project in your area of interest? What standards and guidelines might be employed?

Notes

1. https://www.achp.gov/sites/default/files/regulations/2017-02/regs-rev04.pdf.
2. https://www.nps.gov/history/howto/PAToolkit/consult.htm.
3. The international minerals company Rio Tinto has produced a pretty good (I think) set of guidelines promoting culturally sensitive consultation that may be persuasive to some clients. See http://www.riotinto.com/documents/ReportsPublications/Rio_Tinto_Cultural_Heritage_Guide.pdf.

4. https://ich.unesco.org/en/home.
5. https://www.linguisticsociety.org/content/endangered-languages.
6. My good friend Connie Ramirez has told me about getting her start in local plan-ning, back in the 1960s, mapping culturally valued smells—of coffee shops and spaghetti houses—in San Francisco.
7. Cf. https://en.wikipedia.org/wiki/Community_organizing.
8. https://munsell.com/.
9. See, for example, https://www.nrcs.usda.gov/wps/portal/nrcs/detail/soils/edu/?cid=nrcs142p2_054311.
10. If you're new to rock art, a pretty good place to start is http://thinkingmuse.com/rock-art-petroglyphs/.
11. Cf. https://en.wikipedia.org/wiki/Traditional_ecological_knowledge.

Further Reading

Consultation/Negotiation

Cleese, John, et al. n.d. *Decisions, Decisions.* http://www.videoarts.com/vintage-video-arts/decisions-decisions/.
> A perfectly lovely video about the necessity and art of consultation en route to decision making (or "taking," in the UK).

Cohen, Raymond. 1997. *Negotiating Across Cultures: International Communication in an Interdependent World.* Rev. ed. Washington, DC: United States Institute of Peace Press.
> Cohen's focus is on international diplomacy, but his recommendations are entirely relevant to consultation and negotiation in CRM where differing cul-tures, ethnicities, and worldviews are involved.

Fisher, Roger, William Ury, and Bruce Patton. 2011. *Getting to Yes: Negotiating Agree-ment without Giving In.* Rev. ed. New York: Penguin Books.
> The grandparent of books on negotiation. Cohen rightly criticizes it for lacking sensitivity to cultural differences, but it still provides a tremendous amount of helpful guidance.

Government Accountability Office (GAO). 2019. *Tribal Consultation: Additional Fed-eral Actions Needed for Infrastructure Projects.* GAO-19-22. 20 March. https://www.gao.gov/assets/700/697694.pdf.
> A United States government critique of consultation practices among govern-ment agencies. Although focused on tribal consultation, it is relevant to con-sultation with all sorts of parties.

Nissley, Claudia, and Thomas F. King. 2014. *Consultation and Cultural Heritage: Let Us Reason Together.* New York: Routledge.
> Our attempt to adapt general principles of consultation/negotiation to the specifics of CRM, especially under Section 106 of the National Historic Pres-ervation Act.

Ury, William. 1993. *Getting Past No: Negotiating in Difficult Situations*. New York: Bantam Books.
> The counterweight to Fisher, Ury, and Patton. What to do if your negotiations go off the tracks.

Identification

Berkes, Fikret. 2017. *Sacred Ecology*. 4th ed. New York: Routledge.
> A widely used book about traditional ecological knowledge (TEK).

Menzies, Charles R., ed. 2006. *Traditional Ecological Knowledge and Natural Resource Management*. Lincoln: University of Nebraska Press.
> Another valuable TEK primer.

UNESCO. n.d. "What Is Intangible Cultural Heritage?" https://ich.unesco.org/en/what-is-intangible-heritage-00003.
> The UNESCO Convention on "intangible cultural heritage" is the major international standard that addresses this type of cultural resource.

UNESCO. n.d. "World Heritage List." http://whc.unesco.org/en/list.
> On the international stage, signatories to the World Heritage Convention nominate places perceived to have outstanding heritage importance, including cultural places, to the WHL.

United States Congress, Library of. n.d. "Historic American Buildings Survey/Historic American Engineering Record/Historic American Landscapes Survey." http://www.loc.gov/pictures/collection/hh/.
> You can review what's been recorded by the acronymous National Park Service "survey" programs—HABS, HAER, and HALS—on this site.

United States National Park Service. 1977. "Guidelines for Local Surveys: A Basis for Preservation Planning." *National Register Bulletin* 24. https://www.nps.gov/nr/publications/bulletins/nrb24/.
> Aimed particularly at local governments and non-professionals in the United States, these guidelines encourage systematic identification of historic districts, sites, buildings, structures, and objects. Last revised in 1985, it is a little dated.

United States National Park Service. n.d. "Secretary of the Interior's Standards for Identification." https://www.nps.gov/history/local-law/arch_stnds_2.htm.
> The Secretary's "Standards for Identification" lay out broad recommendations for the identification of historic properties, but *not* for other types of cultural resource.

White, Gregory G., and Thomas F. King. (2007) 2016. *The Archaeological Survey Manual*. New York: Routledge.
> Our effort to outline methods for conducting archaeological survey as a part of historic property and cultural resource identification.

Chapter 3

What CRM Archaeologists Do
Evaluation

What Does It Mean?

Having found something, you almost always have to *evaluate* it somehow. This doesn't mean—or at least very seldom means—figuring out its value in monetary terms. It means trying to figure out how important it is, and what, if anything, makes it important.

Of course, the thing may have already been evaluated and perhaps included in some official list (like the NRHP in the United States). If so, fine, but you need to think about whether its evaluation was accurate, complete, and comprehensive. For example, a building may have been determined to be historically significant, but what about the ground underneath and around it? Could it be an archaeological site? And if the building itself was found significant as an example of some particular architectural style, or for association with a particular historical event, are there other aspects of significance that need to be considered? What have people done in the building? What do they do there now? What values do they ascribe to it?

Similar questions need to be asked if the place was evaluated in the past and found to have *no* historic or cultural significance. You need to consider how long ago the evaluation was done, and whether it was done well or poorly. For example, have new research questions developed that give significance to an archaeological site evaluated two decades ago as worthless? And did that 20-year-old archaeological evaluation consider the site's possible *non*-archaeological values—like its importance to a local community?

In short, don't assume that no evaluation needs to be done just because the place was evaluated sometime in the past.

Evaluation versus Listing

By "evaluation," I mean the more or less pure intellectual process of figuring out what significance something has. This may or may not lead to formal entry onto an official list or "schedule," which (in the United States at least) is a tedious, ponderous, mind-deadening business that usually serves little real-world purpose. Please understand: one can *evaluate* without trying to *list*, that is, without filling out the bloody forms. Unless you're forced to—which may well happen but ought to be questioned.

Bias and Subjectivity

Ideally, evaluation is done in an *unbiased* manner, without reference to its implications for the project or land management activity that's caused you to evaluate it. If recognizing that a cultural resource is important will throw a monkey wrench into your client's plans to build something or your agency's management priorities, that should be utterly irrelevant to your evaluation. When planning a moon mission, we don't assume that the moon is closer than it is so as to save fuel, and when planning a project that will affect cultural resources, we don't assume that those resources are unimportant so as to save our client money or time or trouble. Of course, the significance of a place or thing in cultural terms is a lot less cut and dried than the round-trip mileage to the moon, but the principle remains that we evaluate without considering how that evaluation may affect what our client or employer wants to do. This can sometimes be a rather hard principle for clients and those who work for them (like your supervisors) to embrace, but it's absolutely crucial to CRM practice.

By saying that the evaluation has to be unbiased, I don't mean that only *objective* criteria or objectively defined variables must or even can be taken into account. The significance of a cultural resource—be it a historic place or something else—is almost always more or less subjective. Even famous, widely accepted cultural resources like the Parthenon, the Taj Mahal, or the Golden Gate Bridge are usually described in subjective terms reflecting aesthetic considerations and their perceived places in history. This is pretty much always the case.

And to an extent, we can't avoid a degree of bias in *favor* of cultural resources. Most of us wouldn't be in the business if we didn't think that cultural resources (however we define them) are important. We need to be aware of this bias as we carry out and document our evaluations, and be sensitive to how it's likely to be perceived by others.

Peeking around Professional Blinders

We also need to be aware that our perceptions and biases structure what we even *recognize* as cultural resources. I know, you're probably sick of my railing about how archaeologists tend to recognize as "cultural" only archaeological sites and their contents, but the problem of bias is not exclusive to archaeologists. Architectural historians tend to recognize only buildings and structures and their architectural elements as cultural. Art historians tend to give pride of place to works of art, and so on. This is natural and not unreasonable as long as you're not pretending to evaluate cultural resources in general. But when your responsibility *is* to evaluate cultural resources in general, then you really need to look beyond the blinders set up by your own professional expertise. Doing this can be a challenge, and since it's likely that your client or employer will *expect* you to evaluate all kinds of cultural resources—because surely that's what a cultural resource manager does, isn't it?—you may simply not have the luxury of remaining within your disciplinary box. If you can bring in experts representing different disciplines who are able to look at the situation from different points of view, that's great. But chances are you'll have to consider those points of view yourself.

Evaluating Historic Places

In the United States, there's no established, agreed-upon system for evaluating "cultural resources" in general. There *is* a widely understood (if disputed) system for evaluating "historic places"—also called "historic properties" and "historic resources"—described by the NHPA as "any district, site, building, structure, or object that is included in or eligible for inclusion in the National Register." This is a federal system that's used throughout the country, and identical or similar systems have been put in place by many states, tribes, and local governments. As a CRM practitioner, at least above the lowest journeyman level, you'll be expected to know about this system in considerable detail.

"Districts, sites, buildings, structures, and objects" are all *tangible things*— usually, though not always, pieces of real estate. This does not mean, or should not mean, that you can ignore cultural resources that don't happen to be so tangible. But first let's look at historic places, whose identification, evaluation, and management tend to dominate a CRM practitioner's time.

The Categories

First, let's talk about what those terms mean: "districts, sites, buildings, structures, and objects."

Sites. We can begin by cherry-picking the term that's most familiar to archaeologists: "site." To most archaeologists, a site is the location of some interesting past human activity; it's usually the place where we dig or conduct other kinds of research. That's fine as far as it goes, but "site" can mean something else to people who are *not* archaeologists. For example, consider the location, deep in a forest, high on a mountain, or in a canyon someplace, where a spiritual person goes to pray or seek visions or make medicine. There may be nothing there for an archaeologist to study, but surely it is still a "site." Or to use a sillier example, consider the isolated bridge in the rural neighborhood where I grew up, where teenagers used to get together on long summer evenings to drink illicit beer, tell dirty stories, and make out if they could. This too is certainly a site. Not to my way of thinking a culturally important site, but a "site" nonetheless.

The National Park Service, which of course oversees the National Register of Historic Places (NRHP), has defined "site" as "the location of a significant event, a prehistoric or historic occupation or activity, or a building or structure, whether standing, ruined, or vanished, where the location itself maintains historical or archeological value regardless of the value of any existing structure."[1] This definition has some built-in ambiguities. It requires one to decide whether some past event was "significant" even before deciding that the place where the event occurred is a "site." Similarly, it requires one to determine whether a "location itself" has "historical or archaeological value" before deciding whether it's a site. So is the place where the religious practitioner practices "significant" enough to make it a site? Does it have historical value? Presumably, it is and does in the eyes of the religious practitioner, but does someone *else* have to recognize it is significant or valuable? I'd say "no," but the Park Service is silent on this question.

Rather than chasing one's tail too long using the Park Service definition, it may be better to think of the word "site" the way Webster's dictionary defines it—as "the place where anything is fixed; situation; local position; as, the site of a city or of a house."

Both of our examples meet this definition. The place where the religious practitioner practices is the place where his or her practice is fixed. The place where the kids drink beer and neck is the place they have fixed upon to do so. The square meter or so of floor encompassing the chair on which I'm sitting as I type these words also meets the dictionary definition. We can recognize each as a "site" without having to scratch our heads over whether it's significant.

But there is some practical merit in employing the Park Service definition, at least in a rough and ready kind of way. Arguably, every square meter of the Earth's surface is the "site" where *something* is fixed, even if that something is only the dirt filling the square meter, but in the CRM business, we're concerned about places and things that have some crack at being culturally significant. So using the Park Service definition is probably OK, provided we keep its inherent circularity in mind, and keep our minds open to the possibility that something about *any* place we're looking at may be thought significant and historically valuable by *somebody*.

Neither the Webster nor the Park Service definition limits how big a "site" can be, nor does either of them specify that it has to have clearly marked boundaries. Practically speaking, though, a site for NRHP purposes can't be too monstrously huge, and it ought to have some sort of reasonably recognizable limits.

Obviously, archaeological sites are "sites" for purposes of the NRHP. The thing to remember, however, is that they're not the *only* things that may be sites. You've got to keep the spiritual practitioner and the partying teenagers in mind when you're deciding whether what you found out in the field constitutes a "site."

Even with respect to a site that *is* archaeological—that is, that *does* contain some expression of human activity that an archaeologist might study—the way you as an archaeologist define the site may be very different from the way someone else defines it. In California, where I did a lot of archaeological work decades ago, it was common for us to define sites based on the leavings of human activity that we could recognize on the surface or through test excavation. These leavings usually comprised what we called "middens," made up of ashy, chemically altered soil with lots of fire-cracked rocks, marine shells, bones, artifacts, and often the remains of prehistoric houses, public buildings, and graves. But to the indigenous people whose ancestors had lived there, the site might be better defined in terms of its relationship to a stream, to oak groves or mesquite thickets, or to rock outcrops that could serve as lookouts, seed-grinding stations, safe storage locations, or places for spiritual practice. An archaeologist might not be able to learn anything from the stream, the grove or thicket, or the rock outcrop, but that would not mean that they were not part of the site as understood by those most closely related to it.

Ideally, what we call a "site" should include *both* those of its aspects that appear important to the people who value it *and* those that appear important to archaeologists and other outside specialists.

Districts. If a place is too big to be a site, or too complicated, it may be a "district." As used by the NRHP, a district is "a geographically definable area, urban or rural, possessing a significant concentration, linkage, or continuity of sites, buildings, structures, or objects united by past events or aesthetically by plan or physical development." The term "district" first came into the historic preservation lexicon as a name for places that contained more than one historically or architecturally interesting building or structure—for example, urban neighborhoods and industrial precincts. The term soon came to be recognized as relevant to rural areas too, for example, a river valley containing multiple farms or ranches. In the 1970s and 1980s, when indigenous groups in the United States and elsewhere got seriously involved in historic preservation and insisted that their cultural places be given the same consideration as those valued by dominant ethnic communities, the term came to be applied to landscapes that might show little or no evidence of human activity or modification—a mountain, for example, or a lake and its shoreline, or a river valley whose river, trees, springs, bogs, wildlife, and plants constitute the "significant concentration, linkage, or continuity of sites" that make the district "definable."

Because the meaning of the term "district" has evolved through time, people get into a lot of dumb arguments about it, and about whether a given place does or does not meet the term's definition. Just as scholars, jurors, and politicians in the United States organize themselves into "originalist" and "non-originalist" camps with respect to the United States Constitution, CRM practitioners, SHPOs, and government agency officials may bind themselves tightly or loosely to the original language of the regulatory definition, and to the way that language was originally interpreted in the 1960s and 1970s. Suppose, for example, that we have a 1,000 square mile river valley where an indigenous group has lived, hunted, gathered, and fished for the last two thousand years. Can this valley be regarded as a district? An originalist might say no, the valley is just too big, and it contains no buildings or structures or even sites that an outside analyst can identify as constituting significant concentrations, linkages, or continuities. A non-originalist can counter that the Park Service definition does not impose size limits, and does not require that the "sites, buildings, structures, or objects" contained in a district be definable by outside parties. From the standpoint of the indigenous community, the places where elk are commonly taken by traditional hunters may be important "sites." So may all the places where elk browse, mate, and give birth to their young, all the springs where pure water can be gathered, and all the bogs where plants can be obtained for basketmaking and medicinal purposes. Hunting blinds and traps may be regarded as important "structures." Elk, birds, fish, and trees may be important "objects." A non-originalist can even point out that to deny the legitimacy of these sites, structures, and objects, and therefore the district of which they are a part, would be an act of environmental injustice that might raise litigable civil rights issues.

I am an unapologetic non-originalist. I think that those who wrote the National Park Service guidance on the subject of districts were human beings just like you and me. (I knew or know a lot of them personally, and they certainly *seem* human.) They wrote their guidance based on the cases and issues that were before them at the time, reflecting their knowledge and professional biases, but they were guided by a basic principle—*that what people value in the environment for historic and cultural reasons ought to be respected by those in power*. We ought not to use the National Register to enshrine the places valued by mainstream "majority" social groups at the expense of those valued by people with less political and economic power.

So my recommendation, as usual, is that you find and talk to the people who care about the place, and try to translate their concerns into language that makes sense to the CRM authorities—which in the United States usually means relating their concerns somehow to the NRHP. If they say that the river valley in which they and their ancestors have fished, gathered plants, and hunted elk is important to them, then you probably ought to call it a district.

The NRHP definition goes on to say that a district "may also comprise individual elements separated geographically but linked by association or history." This peculiar language was included to make it possible to nominate "discontiguous districts" to the Register. I don't recall who thought this would be a good idea, or why, but it came to pass sometime in the late 1970s. The idea was that you might have several distinct areas that were related somehow but didn't share boundaries—maybe the steamboat docks on the river and the homes of the steamboat owners up on the bluff—and you'd nominate them all together. This may be useful as part of the administrative act of nomination, but I've never understood its utility as an aspect of evaluation.

Structures and buildings. A "structure," according to the NRHP, is "a work made up of interdependent and interrelated parts in a definite pattern of organization. Constructed by man, it is often an engineering project large in scale." A building is "a structure created to shelter any form of human activity, such as a house, barn, church, hotel, or similar structure. Building may refer to a historically related complex such as a courthouse and jail or a house and barn."

So a structure is something that human beings construct, and it's a building if they construct it in order to shelter some kind of activity. A bridge is a structure, as is a battleship or an airplane, but they're not regarded as buildings (never mind that they all "shelter ... human activity," at least temporarily). A mound or earthwork is a structure (though it may also be a site). A house is a building; so is a barn, a church, St. Peter's Basilica.

Objects. Finally, an "object," to the NRHP, is "a material thing of functional, aesthetic, cultural, historical or scientific value that may be, by nature or design, movable yet related to a specific setting or environment." Luckily, very few "objects" are ever evaluated as eligible (or ineligible) for the NRHP, because the definition is sort of a mess.

For one thing, though an object may be "movable," it had better not be *too* movable. If you can pick it up and put it in your pocket, it's unlikely to be welcomed as eligible for the NRHP. In fact, most NRHP-listed "objects" are *not* movable; they're things like street lamps and statues—except statues aren't ordinarily eligible.

For another thing, this definition—like the one for "site"—includes all those weaselly "value" words: "functional, aesthetic, cultural, historical or scientific." So if an object—say, that chair on the other side of the room—doesn't have any of those values, is it not an "object"? Is it going to dematerialize? Poof? Well, of course not, but all those words provide lots of opportunities for hair-splitting arguments. Luckily, we seldom get into them, because few things are ever considered to be objects that might be eligible for the NRHP.

Trees are among the "objects" that *have* on occasion been regarded as eligible for the NRHP, and in 2005 federal litigation,[2] the court opined that an animal might be eligible on the same basis. No one has done much with these possibilities, although trees, other plants, and animals are pretty routinely identified as "elements" that "contribute" to the significance of historic sites, districts (especially landscapes), buildings, and structures.

Of course, there are things that ride the uncomfortable boundary between defined classes. For example, a ship is normally regarded as a structure, but what about a canoe? Structure or object? Or what if it's embedded in a river-bank? Then is it a site?

What about an old automobile? Is it an NRHP kind of object, or is it too movable? Does that depend on the condition of its tires? What if there are three old cars collapsing into rust together; are they structures, or a site?

Or what about an airplane? The NRHP generally doesn't list museum speci-mens, but is the bright red Lockheed Vega in which Amelia Earhart soloed across the Atlantic in 1932 not eligible because it's in the United States National Air and Space Museum? If it is eligible, what about a half-restored Curtis Jenny in an air museum in southwest Kansas? And what about a crashed airplane? Structure? Site? Or what?

Integrity

To be eligible for the NRHP, say its regulations, a place must "possess integrity of location, design, setting, materials, workmanship, feeling, and association."[3] NRHP specialists often wax sanctimonious about the importance of having integrity. What exactly the word means is anybody's guess, and often it's taken to mean whatever the official "expert" evaluating a place decides it means. The regulations are silent on the begged question of in whose eyes a place must "possess integrity." The potential for ethnocentric bias here is immense.

I don't suppose we could live without some notion like integrity, but I don't think we ought to get all wrapped up in it. It seems to me that if the people who value a place think it has integrity, then it is no business of yours or mine or some highfalutin government authority to say it doesn't. If they say it doesn't have integrity and we think it does—for instance, if we think an archaeologi-cal site is suitable for research but the people associated with it say it's worth-less—then we should certainly offer our arguments, which should be duly considered in the evaluation process. But they shouldn't be privileged above those of the local people, and neither should those of the "official authorities." Nor should those of the locals over ours. It ought all to be negotiable.

The Levels

Places can be eligible for the NRHP at the "national," "state," and/or "local" levels. These distinctions are effectively meaningless, except that every now and then, some member of Congress will bloviate about how we really need to pay more attention to places purported to have "national significance" (which can be listed in the NRHP as "National Historic Landmarks") than to those of "merely local significance." The elitist, antidemocratic character of this notion should be enough to make any citizen gag, but the NRHP takes it seriously enough to maintain checkboxes on its nomination forms. If one is filling out such a form, checking one box or another doesn't make an iota of difference to how the place you're evaluating is considered, except that if you say it's nationally significant it'll get more chin-rubbing scrutiny by professional nit-pickers. So I recommend *not* checking the "national significance" checkbox.

The Criteria

Having decided whether you're dealing with a district, site, building, structure, or object, you're supposed to apply certain "criteria" to decide whether it's eligible for the NRHP. That is, this is what you do in the United States. Each other nation has its own system, and many of them are probably a lot less bizarre than the one we use. I'm going to have to lapse here into some pretty esoteric blather, which will be meaningful only to those working in the United States, so I beg my non-American readers to pardon me. You may want to skip the next few pages, or just prepare to endure a lot of eye-rolling.

There are four NRHP criteria. If your property meets any *one* of them, it's eligible to be put on the list. But that doesn't mean you have to nominate it and get it listed. It's *really important to remember* that under United States federal law, what matters is that a property is *eligible* for the NRHP—*not* that it is actually *included* (that is, listed). Section 106 of the NHPA says that federal agencies must consider the effects of their proposed actions both on places included in the NRHP and those eligible for inclusion—that is, those that meet the NRHP criteria. As far as federal law is concerned—and we can thank the late president Richard M. Nixon for this—nobody seeking to make sure that a place is considered by a federal agency in planning an action has to go through the pain and misery of nominating the place to the NRHP, put up the money to do so, or expose themselves to the idiotic interrogation of those who supervise the oh-so-serious business of nominating stuff to the precious list. Under state and local law, nomination sometimes (but not always) *is* necessary, but not under federal law.

The folks who run the NRHP will assure you that nomination is a *good thing to do*, and a lot of CRM consultants make money preparing nominations. But as far as federal law is concerned—that is, Section 106 of the NHPA—it just isn't necessary. There are other reasons for listing—for example, getting tax breaks for rehabilitating a building—and it's often a politically attractive thing to do. Still, my recommendation is to avoid doing it, in all its expensive, frustrating tedium, *unless* you establish that there really is a practical reason for doing so.

That said, *eligibility* for the NRHP *is* important and worth demonstrating. A place is eligible if it meets any *one* of the NRHP criteria—which are set forth in regulation at 36 CFR 60.4. There are four criteria, labeled "A" through "D."[4]

Criterion A (Association)

A place is eligible if it is "associated with events that have made a significant contribution to the broad patterns of our history." "History" is understood to include not only written history but oral history and human prehistory—the time before written records, but not before human beings were present on the scene.[5] Exactly how tight or integral the association has to be is something that people argue about, along with the nature of the evidence necessary to demonstrate association and indeed even what qualifies as an "event." Generally speaking, "events" are understood to include specific happenings at particular places (e.g., the assassination of a president) and general processes implying multiple events (e.g., the domestication of animals). But people argue about such things.

Obvious examples of Criterion A properties include:

- battlefields associated with—well, battles, that played roles in history;
- industrial facilities or laboratories associated with the invention or development of important products or processes of manufacture, or with scientific discoveries;
- places where important treaties were negotiated or signed;
- places where important civic demonstrations, speeches, and even riots took place; and
- the sites of major catastrophes like floods, fires, explosions, and mine collapses.

Yes, I've used modifiers rather giddily in the above examples. What makes a treaty or a speech or a catastrophe "important" or "major"? I don't know, and I doubt if it's possible to say, but it's something to think about when applying this criterion—or any of the criteria. The importance or frivolity of a place's associations may be clear and easily understood, but they also may not, and you may have to argue for your interpretation.

It seems to me (but to very few others) that virtually any site we think important for archaeological research is eligible under Criterion A. After all, if the site's not associated with "broad patterns of our history"—like, say, the development of a prehistoric group's ways of life—why do we think it's worth study? If we *do* think it's worth study, then surely it at least hypothetically has such associations.

Archaeologists often get wrapped up in Criterion A with respect to "TCPs"—that is, "traditional cultural properties" or, the preferred term since about 1992, "traditional cultural places."[6] A TCP is a place whose significance lies in how it's perceived by a community with reference to that community's identity and valued traditions (remember Merriam-Webster's definition of "community"). The classic example is a place that an indigenous group associates with its spiritual beliefs—the place where the cosmic snake emerged from the ground, or where all the ancestral animals turned to stone. Or as a more homely example, the place where people have gone for a long time to gather willows for basketmaking or berries for making jam.

When an archaeologist is asked about a place that might be a TCP, he or she may answer that its cultural association needs to be demonstrated with some kind of physical, documentary, or artifactual evidence—that there's got to be something that looks to the archaeologist, or to some reputable ethnographer or historian, like a cosmic snake, or there have to be tools in the ground that people have used for willow gathering or berry picking. But that—let me say without mincing words—strikes me as narrow-minded, ethnocentric, and borderline racist. The archaeologist is saying that the place has to meet his or her standards of physical proof in order to be given respect and consideration. Yet anthropology, the discipline in which archaeology (in the United States) resides, has a vast literature of ethnographic and ethnohistorical data, distinguishable from the oral histories of indigenous (and other) communities only by having been written down mostly by white men and the occasional woman. It would be a rare archaeologist—at least in the United States—who would not regard those data as admissible evidence of association. Why should a community's *own* record of its believed traditions be insufficient to demonstrate "association with significant events" just because no outside analyst has written them down? I think that's deplorable.

Criterion B (Big People)

A place is eligible if it's "associated with the lives of persons significant in our past." According to the NRHP, this does not mean places where important people got born or buried, unless the person did something else there as well or unless there's no place associated with that person's productive life (how one is supposed to prove such a negative is a mystery to me). We're talking here about the place where a political leader gave a pivotal speech, or the place where somebody wrote an important book or invented something. Such a place might also be eligible under Criterion A, which is OK; there's no rule against judging something eligible under multiple criteria.

Here again, I've used weaselly words—"pivotal" and "important." Here again, importance may be arguable, and not obvious. And remember, always, that local significance is just as good as national significance when it comes to NRHP eligibility. So the association of the old privy pit with Mayor Grump may be quite sufficient to make it eligible for the NRHP, even though the mayor never got to be governor or president.

Criterion C (Characteristics, Cute Buildings, or Catch-All)

A place is eligible if it embodies "distinctive characteristics of a type, period, or method of construction" or represents "the work of a master," possesses "high artistic values," or represents "a significant and distinguishable entity whose components may lack individual distinction." This criterion is something of a mess, but it's very important to architectural historians because it's the criterion that captures representatives of architectural styles. If a place exemplifies Classical Revival or Richardsonian Romanesque architecture, it's probably eligible under Criterion C. But Criterion C goes way beyond formal architectural styles; it references "periods" and "types" and "methods," so there's lots of room for buildings and structures (and in theory, other kinds of places) that don't fit into particular styles. "Vernacular" architecture—reflecting the informal building practices and styles of a community or group—can be eligible under Criterion C, and so can other kinds of built stuff.

How about "the work of a master"? That can be a master architect, landscape architect, engineer, builder, shipwright, carpenter, or—presumably—plumber or computer designer. And yes, it can include anonymous "masters" like those who may be inferred to have designed a prehistoric structure or road system.

Then there's "high artistic values," which of course can be reflected in a building's ornamentation and symbolic art and in the artistry of landscape design. Less formal kinds of art can fit under this criterion as well—for example, indigenous petroglyphs, pictographs, and totem poles.

Finally, there's that "significant and distinguishable entity whose components may lack individual distinction." Suppose you have an urban neighborhood made up of really boring little houses, but it turns out that there was a period in the architectural history of the area when boring little houses were the very height of fashion, and this neighborhood is an especially pure example of the type—there's not a house in the bunch that's individually interesting. The neighborhood might be eligible as a "distinguishable entity" under Criterion C; it'd be called a "district."

The "distinguishable entity" subcriterion can apply to archaeological sites as well (among other things). Say, for example, that you have a big alluvial fan on which nodules of flint are scattered, and at various times in antiquity people briefly gathered around and worked on nodules to produce tools, leaving scatters of flint flakes, hammerstones, and maybe antler tools used in fine pressure-flaking. Any individual scatter might "lack distinction," but the overall "entity"—the alluvial fan—would be "distinguishable," so it might qualify as an NRHP-eligible district or site. A traditional cultural landscape may constitute a distinguishable NRHP-eligible district too, usually under both Criteria C and A.

Criterion D (Data or Dig)

A place is eligible if it has "yielded, or may be likely to yield, information important in prehistory or history." It's under Criterion D that most archaeological sites and site complexes are determined eligible, and the temptation for an archaeologist is simply to ignore all the other criteria. That's understandable, but dangerous, because it's possible (stupid, but possible) to argue that if a place is eligible only under Criterion D, it's easy to extract the data from it and preserve those data in a museum or in the pages of a book or in a piece of software, whereupon the place that originally contained the data is no longer significant and can be blown away with impunity. Of course, there are all kinds of things wrong with this notion, as any archaeologist should know. Methods evolve, discoveries are made, new hypotheses are advanced that require the application of new tools. And once a site has been destroyed, there's no way to apply new thinking to its study. Moreover, what an archaeologist thinks is good only for research may be good for much more from the standpoint of non-archaeologists. Without burying ourselves in these details, just note the warning: the temptation to apply only Criterion D to a place should be resisted.

But if you do want to apply Criterion D, how do you do it? Well, if a place *has* yielded information, it should be documented somewhere—usually in the local, regional, or other literature, which you should find during background research. But the *potential* to yield—that "may be likely" stuff—can only be inferred, and the process of inference is a complex landscape full of slippery slopes covering minefields.

Suppose you've found a site representing where someone camped 500 years ago while hunting sea cows. Suppose that over the last few decades, two thousand similar sites have been excavated in the neighborhood and have yielded lots of information on ancient sea cow hunting practices. Are the data you might get from this site therefore not worth getting? Is there no potential for the site to yield important information? I don't have an answer to this question; I just pose it for your consideration—with the understanding that your client very probably will prefer for you to say that the site has no such potential.

Incidentally, I know some would say that the information from the two-thousand-first sea cow hunting site is "redundant" with the data from the previous two thousand. I suggest that you be careful about buying into this assumption. "Redundant" with reference to what? With respect to what hypothesis or body of information? In whose eyes? Some archaeologists, I think, toss the word "redundant" around altogether too thoughtlessly.

Or suppose you've found a site where it looks like somebody did something in the past—maybe camped, maybe ground some seeds on flat rocks—but based on what you can see on the surface, you can't really be sure *what* they did there, or *when* they did it, or whether whatever they did is "important in prehistory or history." Your natural tendency will probably be to say, "I need to dig some holes in this site to see what it contains." This of course will require time and money, which your client may be reluctant to provide. So do you say, "Well then, based on what I can see on the surface of the ground, I don't think there's important information here," and perhaps let the site be destroyed? Or do you say, "Well, then, based on what I can see, I think there *is* important information here," perhaps thus causing your client's project to be redesigned at great cost? Or do you dig in your heels and insist on being funded to test the site, and risk being fired? Again I have no formula to suggest here; I just pose the matter for consideration.

What I *will* suggest is that you think about those *other* criteria—A through C—and *consult with people* about whether they apply. Does the local indigenous group have traditions that make every sea cow hunting station, or the whole landscape full of such stations, a TCP eligible for the NRHP under Criterion A? Or do they have a tradition associating this particular site with the ancient tradition of the Cosmic Sea Cow, making the site eligible under Criteria A and B? Or does the same group say, "We're really not into sea cow hunting sites, but that marsh over there is full of medicinal plants, and it's where our elders have always gone to collect eelgrass—didn't you know that?" Your client probably needs to preserve the marsh anyhow, in order to comply with clean water requirements, so you might have a win-win situation on your hands—at the expense of the sea cow hunting camp.

This is assuming, of course, that when your client's bulldozers gouge into the hunting site, they don't turn up a sea cow burial replete with decorated pottery and shark tooth necklaces—but that's always a risk.

The "Considerations"

Besides the four NRHP criteria, there are seven "criteria considerations," each describing a situation in which something that you might think would be eligible for the NRHP *isn't* eligible. Except when it *is* eligible. Yes.

It would be much too tedious to go into these "considerations" in detail here. I've discussed them in my 2012 textbook, *Cultural Resource Laws and Practice,* and the Park Service has issued guidance about them that's referenced in the appendix of this book. Suffice to say that per the "considerations":

- a religious property isn't eligible based on whatever religious doctrine it represents, but it *can* be eligible for the role it plays in a group's culture, or for its architecture, or for other reasons;
- a property that's been moved isn't usually eligible unless it's become significant in the location to which it's been moved—or implicitly if it's inherently movable, like a ship;
- a birthplace or grave isn't eligible simply because somebody was born or got buried there—unless it's the only place associated with that somebody, and the somebody is *real* important;
- a cemetery isn't eligible except where it has cultural, historical, or archaeological value (presumably there are cemeteries that lack such values, though I've never encountered one);
- a reconstructed property isn't eligible unless it's a really good reconstruction or has been reconstructed by the National Park Service;
- a commemorative property—a statue of Donald Trump, for example—is not eligible for its association with what it commemorates, though it may be eligible for some other reason; and
- a property that became significant only within the last 50 years isn't eligible unless it's "exceptionally significant."

That last consideration is sometimes called the "50-year rule." People argue about it a great deal. Note that it doesn't mean that the place didn't exist until less than 50 years ago. It means that it didn't *get significant* until less than 50 years ago. Sometimes that's a meaningless distinction; other times it's important.

Applying the 50-year rule can be tricky and sometimes emotional. For example, the site of the World Trade Center in New York City became "exceptionally significant" on 9/11/2001; nobody really had an argument with that. But what about the site of a less famous recent event that was exceptionally significant in the life of a community, and whose fate can elicit strong emotions? Who gets to decide?

Well, ultimately, the Keeper of the National Register—that is, the NPS official who oversees management of the NRHP—gets to decide, as was the case even with the World Trade Center. Is that democratic? Is there a rational alternative? Your opinion is as good as mine.

Little Things

It's not a criteria consideration, but it is long-standing NRHP policy that little things aren't eligible. Essentially, if you can (in theory) pick the thing up and walk away with it, it's not eligible. Every now and then someone will challenge this unwritten rule, usually with reference to a museum collection, but the challenge peters out in bureaucratic mush. If you can *drive* the thing away, as in the case of a ship or an airplane, then it's OK—although the people who oversee the Register have trouble with automobiles—but museum collections or other portable artifacts, no.

Little things may be subject to consideration and even protection under a law other than the NHPA—for example, the National Environmental Policy Act (NEPA) and Native American Graves Protection and Repatriation Act (NAGPRA)—and even the NHPA provides for federal agencies to attend to standards issued by the Secretary of the Interior in managing collections of artifacts. But strictly with reference to the NRHP, and hence to consideration under the Section 106 regulations, little things are pretty much left out.

Living Things

It's sometimes said that living things aren't eligible for the NRHP, but this isn't true. Quite a few living trees are listed on the NRHP, and others have been found eligible. No animals have been individually listed or found eligible (as of 2019), but in that obscure case I mentioned earlier—*Dugong v. Rumsfeld*, adjudicated in California but dealing with animals in Japan—the court opined that animals might be eligible as "objects." The NRHP has studiously avoided responding to this opinion.

Bulletins, "Historic Contexts," etc.

During the 1970s and 1980s, when questions arose about how to interpret the NRHP criteria, the National Park Service started publishing "bulletins" about how to evaluate different kinds of places. See the section titled "Further Reading" at the end of this chapter for some of the most useful. The bulletins were well-intended efforts, I think, but most were aimed at helping people complete

NRHP nomination forms—an activity that's pretty marginal to most CRM work, and to the real world in general. There was also little effort to coordinate the various bulletins, so some of them wound up seeming to contradict others.

In the early 1980s, too, the NPS decided that evaluation would be improved if people—professionals and government officials, of course—developed "historic contexts." These were state-based, or occasionally regional, overviews of some type or types of property, which reviewed relevant history and prehistory, environmental variables, and so on, resulting in putatively logical systems within which actual properties, real places, could be evaluated.

One problem with the "contexts" was that they tended to be very abstract, academic, and hard to use in the evaluation of actual places. Or—and this has become an increasingly serious problem—they were taken to be Holy Writ; if a place didn't somehow fall within a category identified by a "context" as significant, it simply *wasn't*. And although NPS guidelines more or less encouraged public involvement in context development, it's pretty hard to get people interested in volunteering their time to work on something so abstract. As a result, contexts have mostly been developed by consultants, with input from SHPO staff and sometimes academic historians, architects, and archaeologists.

On the whole, preparation of "contexts" has provided money for a good deal of consultant work, and has sometimes led regional historians, archaeologists, and other specialists to get together and seek agreement about what is and isn't important and why. But my impression is that most "contexts" are pretty useless, and some are flatly counterproductive. Perhaps the worst thing about them—from my admittedly jaundiced point of view—is that they encourage a sort of pseudo-academic, ivory-tower approach to historic preservation that discourages public engagement and relevance to the people who, after all, pay the taxes that make governmental historic preservation possible. So my strong recommendation is to *refer* to any available "contexts" (which may go under other names) as sources of data during your background research, but don't *rely* on them, either as information sources or as ways to structure your evaluation of particular properties. Think for yourself, do your own research. Use the Internet and the library; ferret out sources that may be available in neither place. And critically, *consult* others who may be wiser than you—including colleagues, technical experts, indigenous and descendant groups, and local residents, particularly if you're part of the mainstream ethnicity and the people of the community you're studying were or are not.

In the Rest of the World

I have to confess a deep ignorance of how CRM is done in nations other than the United States, though I've had some contact with practice in Canada, Japan, China, the United Kingdom, Australia, New Zealand, and Fiji. I've never actually *done* CRM outside the jurisdictions of the United States and its associated

Pacific Island governments. Based on what little I do know, and what I've read, including the papers kindly provided by several colleagues and grouped together as chapter 8, my impression is that while evaluation of places and things is a necessary part of CRM everywhere, practitioners outside the United States are not burdened by anything quite as mind-bogglingly contorted as our NRHP.

The categories used by other national systems are often different from those of the NRHP. Rather than "districts, sites, buildings, structures, and objects," you're likely to see reference to things like "monuments," sometimes with precise definitions, sometimes not. Some countries give special consideration to ancient sites in caves, or to temple complexes.

Another difference is that other nations—while employing less contorted evaluation criteria than those of the NRHP—make more of the lists that the application of those criteria produce. In some countries, inclusion in such a list—variously called a "schedule," an "inventory," a "register," or just a plain "list"—is a prerequisite to being considered for preservation or anything like it. In other cases, the lists are reserved for those places that the government intends to preserve and perhaps restore and develop somehow, while other kinds of cultural places, such as most archaeological sites, are dealt with outside the "listing" context. Thus, a "scheduled" castle may be given very substantial legal protection, at least on paper, while an "unscheduled" site found during survey in advance of development will almost invariably be subjected to salvage or "rescue" excavation and then destroyed. We reach the same conclusions in the United States, of course; we just take a different route.

Outside the United States, archaeology is often handled separately and apart from other aspects of "heritage." This may reflect the fact that in much of the world archaeology is a stand-alone academic discipline. But whatever its basis, keeping archaeology separate makes it easier for archaeologists simply to be archaeologists and pretty much ignore concerns that do not involve artifacts and ruins.

Depending on the country, a nation's CRM system may give less or more cognizance to "ethnic" heritage than the United States does. A country like China or Russia, which has heritage lists that operate at both national and regional/provincial/local levels, presumably recognizes the cultural resources of regional ethnic groups rather de facto, but there may be less formal attention to the matter than we in the United States experience. Canada, Australia, New Zealand, and Brazil are in situations roughly similar to that of the United States, with immigrant European populations dominating the political and hence heritage landscape but growing recognition (except lately in Brazil) that those present before the European onslaught have important heritage resources of their own. New Zealand, for example, in common with India, is a leader in recognizing rivers as important heritage places, with their own rights.[7]

In some countries, the CRM/heritage system and the development sectors seem to operate with little reference to each other. In such countries there may be a vigorous program to "schedule" important historic places, to monitor and oversee their maintenance, and even to protect them from unauthorized "looting," while modern development goes on with little attention to its impacts on heritage. Of course, this is often the situation in the United States as well, in those cases where federal law doesn't apply (and often enough where it does).

Finally, international standards, systems, and programs—mostly ignored in the United States—are very important to many other nations. UNESCO,[8] ICOMOS,[9] ICUN,[10] ICAHM,[11] the World Bank,[12] and regional bodies such as the European Union (EU)[13] are all influential (in the case of the EU, relatively determinative in Europe). The World Heritage List[14] is especially important in some countries. UNESCO's Convention for the Safeguarding of the Intangible Cultural Heritage[15] and the United Nations Declaration on the Rights of Indigenous Peoples[16] are also having some impact on CRM—outside the well-guarded borders of the United States.

In general, though, wherever CRM is practiced throughout the world, it is mostly focused on tangible places and typically involves identifying and evaluating resources. It may not employ the odd and esoteric criteria used in the United States, but it always involves *some* criteria, which may be pretty peculiar in their own right.

What about Intangibles?

OK, so in the United States at least, cultural resources that are tangible chunks of the environment—usually pieces of real estate—are generally classified as districts, sites, buildings, structures, or objects, and are evaluated with reference to criteria like those of the NRHP. What about things that are *not* tangible?

Often they're not dealt with at all. The very existence of a relatively organized system like the one built around the NRHP may make it easy to ignore things that can't easily be made to fit under one or more of that system's criteria. So naturally, "intangibles" tend to be ignored.

Recognition that this might be a problem led the bulk of the nations participating in UNESCO to agree in 2003 on the Convention for the Safeguarding of the Intangible Cultural Heritage. Having said that intangible heritage should be safeguarded, however, UNESCO wasn't able to figure out anything more creative to do about it than to make lists of "intangibilities," so at this writing there's an argument going on over whether the French baguette should be entered in the international list. This strikes me as regrettable.

In the United States, we promote folklife festivals, indigenous language programs, and other laudable efforts to encourage respect for and retention of intangible culture, but when it comes to considering intangibles in planning and government decision making, we are woefully out of touch. Impacts on intangible "resources" like language, social institutions, subsistence systems, and belief systems *may* be considered under NEPA, but the odds are against it. If enough people make a fuss about, say, the fact that the proposed mine will make it impossible for people to continue to practice subsistence hunting and gathering, or will conflict with traditional views of how human beings should relate to the universe, or will cause kids to speak English rather than their native language, they *may* be able to force some treatment of the matter into the environmental impact assessment documents prepared on the project. More likely they won't, and even if they do, there's little guarantee that anything will be done about it.

So if you're hired as a CRM specialist in a company or agency, the chances are that you won't have much to do with "intangibles" unless you create your own opportunities/needs to do so. What I think is rather sad and foolish about this, and worth your consideration as a current or potential CRM practitioner, is that the "tangible/intangible" divide is pretty vague. Intangible, you might say. Consider, for example, three cases with which I'm involved as I write this book.

In the case of the Mountain Valley Pipeline project in Virginia, if a proposed natural gas pipeline is built, it will cut through several NRHP-listed and several other NRHP-eligible cultural landscapes, whose principal values involve how they are viewed, experienced, enjoyed, *felt* by their residents and passers-through.

In the case of the Ch'u'itnu watershed in Alaska, the proposal is to put in a surface coal mine in the headwaters of a salmon-spawning stream that's been the lifeblood of a local Native Village for the last millennium. The people of the village fish there, hunt there, gather plants there. They'd like to keep doing all that; they *feel* that the watershed is intrinsic to their identity. The mine company says they'd be so much better off working in the mine.

At Fort Polk in Louisiana, the Army is rounding up and getting rid of wild horses that have occupied the Fort's landscape for decades—some say centuries. They're referred to as "trespass horses," though it's debatable who's trespassed upon whom. People of the area—many of them thrown off their farms by the Army in the 1940s—*feel* that the horses are vital links to their cultural heritage.

In each of these cases there are tangible resources—landscapes made up of dirt, trees, springs, mountains, rivers, fish, moose, horses—but the *values* are intangible, involving how people *feel*. These are values you'll have to deal with if you work in CRM—regardless of whether "intangible" appears in your job description.

Study Questions

1. Think of a place you consider to be historically and culturally interesting that's not on any official list of historic places. Imagine that you're evaluating it with reference to the United States NRHP criteria. Which criteria do you think apply? Why and why not? Do any of the "criteria considerations" apply? Why or why not?
2. Think about a totally "intangible" cultural resource that you think might be important. How would you evaluate it?

Notes

1. The definitions for these terms can be found at https://www.law.cornell.edu/cfr/text/36/60.3.
2. *Okinawa Dugong et al. v. Donald Rumsfeld et al.* See https://coast.noaa.gov/data/Documents/OceanLawSearch/Dugong%20v.%20Rumsfeld_Case%20Summary_PDF.pdf.
3. See 36 CFR § 60.4 at https://www.law.cornell.edu/cfr/text/36/60.4. Internationally with reference especially to the World Heritage List, "authenticity" is sometimes used interchangeably with "integrity," except when it's not. There is much academic tooth-gnashing about how to maintain it/them—whatever it/them is/are.
4. For these four criteria, see 36 CFR § 60.4 at https://www.law.cornell.edu/cfr/text/36/60.4.
5. Non-human paleontological sites are not eligible for the NRHP unless they have some human association—like being the site of a theory-changing paleontological discovery.
6. My late wife and co-author Pat Parker and I called them "traditional cultural properties" in National Register Bulletin 38, the Park Service's 1990 guidance on such things (see https://www.nps.gov/nr/publications/bulletins/nrb38/). Many tribes objected that "properties" smacked of commodification and preferred "places." That works for me, and at last report it did for the NRHP, too.
7. In 2018, Colombia extended similar rights to the Amazon rainforest within its borders, and voters in the US state of Ohio extended the rights of "personhood" to Lake Erie. It is too early to judge how these initiatives—or those of India and New Zealand, for that matter—are likely to work out.
8. United Nations Educational, Scientific, and Cultural Organization. See https://en.unesco.org/.
9. International Council on Monuments and Sites. See https://www.icomos.org/en.
10. International Union for Conservation of Nature. See https://www.iucn.org/. IUCN is becoming increasingly involved in addressing the place of culture, especially indigenous culture, in nature.
11. International Committee on Archaeological Heritage Management. See http://icahm.icomos.org/.
12. See http://www.worldbank.org/en/topic/environment. Ostensibly, the World Bank requires environmental impact assessments on projects it funds, including the consideration of cultural resources.
13. See, for example, http://ec.europa.eu/environment/eia/index_en.htm.
14. See http://whc.unesco.org/en/list.
15. See https://ich.unesco.org/.
16. For more details, see https://www.humanrights.gov.au/publications/un-declaration-rights-indigenous-peoples-1.

Further Reading

Categories, Criteria, Considerations

Hardesty, Donald I., and Barbara J. Little. 2009. *Assessing Site Significance: A Guide for Archaeologists and Historians.* 2nd ed. Walnut Creek, CA: Altamira Press.
>A very archaeological take on how to evaluate archaeological sites in terms of their archaeological significance.

UNESCO World Heritage Centre. n.d. *The Criteria for Selection.* http://whc.unesco.org/en/criteria/.
>These are the criteria for inclusion in the World Heritage List.

United States National Park Service. n.d. *National Register of Historic Places.* https://www.law.cornell.edu/cfr/text/36/part-60.
>These are the regulations in which the categories of phenomena eligible for recognition as "historic properties" in the United States are laid out, along with the criteria for evaluating them as such and the "considerations" that may make them *not* eligible.

Living Things

Birnbaum, Charles A. 1994. *Protecting Cultural Landscapes.* United States National Park Service Preservation Brief 36. https://www.nps.gov/tps/how-to-preserve/briefs/36-cultural-landscapes.htm.
>Identifies plants and animals as parts of cultural landscapes eligible for the United States NRHP.

King, Thomas F. 2006. "Animals and the United States National Register of Historic Places." *Applied Anthropologist* 26(2): 129–36. https://www.academia.edu/4377319/Animals_and_the_United_States_National_Register_of_Historic_Places.
>One of the very few explicit discussions I know of regarding this generally ignored topic.

Okinawa Dugong et al. v. Donald Rumsfeld et al. 2005. WL 522106 (N.D. Cal. 2005). https://coast.noaa.gov/data/Documents/OceanLawSearch/Dugong%20v.%20Rumsfeld_Case%20Summary_PDF.pdf.
>The case in which the court opined that an animal might be classified as an "object" eligible for inclusion in the NRHP.

Bulletins, Historic Contexts, etc.

United States National Park Service. n.d. *How to Apply the National Register Criteria for Evaluation.* https://www.nps.gov/nr/publications/bulletins/nrb15/.
>The main NPS guidance on how to evaluate historic properties (*not* cultural resources). Painfully out of date and oriented toward formal nominations, but it's what there is.

United States National Park Service. n.d. *How to Evaluate a Property within Its Historic Context.* https://www.nps.gov/nr/publications/bulletins/nrb15/nrb15_5.htm.
 This is a piece of "How to Apply the … Criteria," specifically addressing historic contexts. I think it's dreadful, but it's widely used.

United States National Park Service. n.d. *National Register Publications.* https://www.nps.gov/subjects/nationalregister/publications.htm.
 A link to the whole kit and caboodle of NPS bulletins and such.

Intangibles

Anonymous. n.d. *Alternative Intangible Cultural Heritage List.* https://www.facebook.com/AlternativeIntangibleCulturalHeritageList/?hc_ref=ARQ5tKw31MkwyZHRhGT69WzuX2x8PADf9BaA6mYH6Hi23AfveS49ruurWgoeQVRAraY.
 If we must have a list, this is an alternative to the official UNESCO list.

Chapter 4

What CRM Archaeologists Do
Assessing Adverse Effects

You've done background research, you've consulted people, you've done field-work, and you've found and evaluated something that you or others conclude is a "cultural resource." Nobody's shot down your conclusion. What's next?

Well, it depends on whether and how the thing will be affected by what your client or agency proposes to do—and, of course, on what it is.

If nobody's proposing to do anything to whatever you've found, then you probably have nothing more to do (but see "neglect," below). In most cases, however, the only reason anybody's invested in finding and evaluating cultural resources is that some change is being considered, so the question you have to address is, what effects will such a change have?

It's OK to Have Adverse Effects

It's important to understand that—in the United States, at least—federal law doesn't prohibit the destruction of anything, no matter how historically or culturally important it may be. Depending on what the thing is, and very importantly depending on who is concerned about it and how willing and able they are to fight for it, the law may make it *difficult* to destroy the thing, but it does not *prohibit* it. It's important that everybody understands this. Often, people who want to preserve something think that if they get it recognized as eligible for the NRHP or an equivalent, that's the end of the game; they've won. In the United States, that's not true. Conversely, people who want to destroy something often think that if it gets recognized as being culturally significant, they've lost. Under federal law in the United States, that's not true either. Both percep-tions, though—and they're really the same perception—result in tremendous amounts of time and effort and money being spent arguing about whether things are significant, when it would often be in everyone's best interests to accept their significance and try to figure out what to do about it.

In many other countries, and under some local historic preservation laws in the United States, it's different. In these contexts, if something is determined to be significant, and is therefore listed or scheduled, this *does* mean that you can't mess with it. In my opinion—for what it's worth—that's a foolishly inflexible way to write law. It elevates cultural significance above everything else, and almost always results in complicated, centralized, elitist systems for deciding what's "worthy" of being listed. And it's a zero-sum game: one side wins, the other loses—despite the fact that often there are ways for both sides to win, if they can get past demonizing each other. But that's just my opinion, and it's not widely shared.

In any event, if you have something that's culturally significant, and you're working under a law like the NHPA, then what you're supposed to do is sit down and figure out what impacts or effects may result from whatever it is that's proposed. This sets the stage for figuring out what to do about the effects.

Criteria of Adverse Effect

Naturally, there are "criteria of adverse effect" embodied in regulation—in the United States, in the NHPA Section 106 regulations at 36 CFR § 800.5. The regulations say that the federal agency responsible for whatever project or land use is being reviewed has to apply the criteria, in consultation with the SHPO or THPO and other parties. But that really means the agency's CRM staff or somebody's CRM contractors apply them—so you need to know what they say and mean.

The Main Criterion

Despite the common (and regulatory) reference to "criteria," there's really only one criterion of adverse effect in the Section 106 regulations. A proposed action will have an adverse effect if it "may alter, directly or indirectly, any of the characteristics of a historic property that qualify the property for inclusion in the National Register in a manner that would diminish the integrity of the property's location, design, setting, materials, workmanship, feeling, or association." There are some important words and phrases here.

May: Note first that word "may." You don't have to be *sure* something bad will happen. If it's *reasonably possible* that it will, that's enough—it's taken as an adverse effect.

Directly or indirectly: "Directly" refers to what's going to happen right away, right at the scene of the crime, as it were—knocking a wing off a building, or bulldozing up a landscape. "Indirectly" means the adverse effect is likely to happen later or farther away. The building won't be taken care of and will eventually fall down, or the landscape downstream will be eroded away because of changes to the river upstream.

The direct/indirect distinction is often—maybe always—rather indistinct. If you—standing 20 meters from me—shoot me in the head, is that effect somehow indirect because I was standing 20 meters away when you pulled the trigger? Similarly, if an indigenous spiritual place is eroded away within twenty years after construction of a dam several kilometers upstream (as happened to Katamin, the center of the world according to the Karuk Tribe in northern California), is that a direct effect or an indirect one?

It doesn't really matter; we have to address all types of effects.

So the main criterion casts a pretty broad net—but note that you won't know what it catches if you haven't done a good job of scoping at the outset. If all you've looked at is the project footprint, you're going to know only about some of its very *direct* effects. The *less direct* ones—and those that are *cumulative*, which we'll discuss in a moment—will blow right past you.

Historic property. On the other hand, to be an adverse effect under the 106 regulations, an action has to have some potential for altering some kind of *historic property*—district, site, building, structure, or object. If it's "only" going to alter, say, the way people dance or sing, it doesn't count—*unless* they dance on, or sing about, something definable as an NRHP-eligible district, site, building, structure, or object. Which may be eligible *because* they dance on or sing about it.

Diminishing integrity. Moreover, the project or action has to risk diminishing "the integrity of the property's location, design, setting, materials, workmanship, feeling, or association." As you can probably imagine, there's a lot of room among all those words for nitpicking argument. "Integrity" according to whom? "Feeling" as measured how? "Association" with whom or what?

Qualifying characteristics. It gets worse. You're supposed to consider "all qualifying characteristics" of the district, site, building, structure, or object, "including those that may have been identified subsequent to the original evaluation of the property's eligibility for the National Register." Which actually makes sense. If the old building was originally found eligible without considering the archaeological site under it, it would be foolish to ignore the archaeology now just because it wasn't noticed back then. But it's another little twist for people to debate.

Indirect effects. The regulations also say that adverse effects "may include reasonably foreseeable effects caused by the undertaking that may occur later in time, [or] be farther removed in distance." Never mind asking "later than what" or "farther than what?" The regulations don't say. But their language is derived from the NEPA regulations, and amounts to the NEPA definition of "indirect" or "secondary" effect. So it means you have to be alert not only to effects likely to happen right now, right here, but also to those that may occur later on, or at a distance.

Cumulative effects. Finally, the regulations say to look out for effects that are "cumulative." What does that mean?

Merriam-Webster tells us that "cumulative" means "increasing by successive additions." If you weighed 80 kg last year and weigh 100 kg this year, that's a cumulative increase of 20 kg. In the same way, if there used to be 100 archaeological sites in the river valley, and now there are 80, that's a cumulative loss of 20 sites. If your client now proposes to put in a project that will take out 20 sites—above and beyond those that would be lost anyhow—that's a problem, and you shouldn't denigrate it by saying, "Oh well, it's only 20 sites."

Cumulative effects are often the hardest to define, and the ones that people are most concerned about. "When I was a little girl," the old woman says, "we used to have lots and lots of sunflowers—which are associated with our ancestor spirits. Now we have not so many, because of the farming, the roads, the pipelines, the pesticides."

That's a statement about cumulative effects, and if your client's project is going to take out some more sunflowers, it's a problem. On the other hand, of course, maybe your client's project is going to encourage the *growth* of sunflowers—or maybe you could make a minor tweak to the project plans that would cause this to happen, which could be a really good idea.

Anyway, cumulative effects—negative and positive—have to be considered in deciding whether your project or activity will have adverse effects on historic properties overall.

But—the Helpful Examples

Before you tear your hair out over the definition of "adverse effect," be of good cheer: the regulations go right on to offer a series of examples. It's these that most people mean when they refer to the "*criteria* of adverse effect." They're actually not criteria; they're examples, derived from and designed to elucidate the general *criterion*.

The First Example

The first example is "physical destruction of or damage to all or part of the property." If you're going to destroy or damage the place, that's an adverse effect. Duh, you say. Duh, I agree, but of course it's possible to argue about whether a given action is or is not "destructive" or "damaging." Still, the first example is pretty straightforward.

The Second Example

The second example is a good deal more complicated. It's an adverse effect if your project will involve "alteration of a property, including restoration, rehabilitation, repair, maintenance, stabilization, hazardous material remediation, and provision of handicapped access." So it's an adverse effect if you're going to *change* the place—*no matter how justified that change may be*.

But wait, the example continues! It's an adverse effect *only* if it's "not consistent with the Secretary [of the Interior]'s standards for the treatment of historic properties (36 CFR part 68) and applicable guidelines." So what it comes down to is that altering a place is an adverse effect unless it's a *nice* alteration, consistent with standards issued by the Secretary of the Interior.

A great many renovations of historic buildings and structures are carried out following the Secretary's Standards, and hence are found to have no adverse effect under Section 106. The Standards are so commonly used, in fact, that many in the historic architecture business think of them as the law—as legally required. They're not, but it is a fact that following them will—at least in theory—make it relatively easy to move a project forward.

Incidentally, the "Secretary's Standards" referred to above are not the *only* "Secretary's Standards." The Secretary of the Interior has issued standards for many different things, and we refer to a couple of them elsewhere. But these *particular* standards—the Secretary of the Interior's Standards for the Treatment of Historic Properties (36 CFR Part 68)—are probably the most widely used and most often cited.

As an archaeologist, you probably won't be called on to opine with authority on whether and how a given project comports with these Secretary's Standards—unless you're the one and only cultural resource expert on the case. If you find yourself in such a situation, you need to spend serious time with the Standards and with the associated guidelines that the National Park Service has put out, most of which are readily available on line.

The Standards and Guidelines are very stuffily written and not much fun to read, but on the whole they're not unreasonable. Incidentally, although they're called the Standards for the *treatment of historic properties*, that's a misnomer in two respects. The first is that they're largely (though not entirely) focused on the treatment of historic *buildings* and *structures*—not sites, cultural landscapes, and other non-built things. The other is that they don't embrace the most common "treatment" of historic buildings and structures—their demolition. I think doing so would be desirable, but it would doubtless offend many preservation advocates.

The Standards are divided into four parts, each dealing with a particular kind of treatment:

- "Preservation," which means keeping the place as it was in the past.
- "Rehabilitation," which means retaining the place's main character-defining elements while adapting it for modern uses. This is by far the most common treatment (other than demolition), and—because rehabilitation per the Standards can qualify a property owner or developer for tax credits—there's a substantial industry that's developed around interpreting and applying them.

- "Restoration," which means pretty much the same as rehabilitation but with emphasis on bringing the place back to what it looked like at an earlier time.
- "Reconstruction," which means building something new that purports to look (and perhaps feel, sound, and smell) just like something old.

In each category, between six and ten standards are prescribed. Here are a couple of them from the "Rehabilitation" category, just to give you a taste:

- Distinctive materials, features, finishes and construction techniques or examples of craftsmanship that characterize a property will be preserved.
- Deteriorated historic features will be repaired rather than replaced. Where the severity of deterioration requires replacement of a distinctive feature, the new feature will match the old in design, color, texture and, where possible, materials. Replacement of missing features will be substantiated by documentary and physical evidence.

Obviously, there's a lot of room for interpretation, and your colleagues in historic architecture can debate such interpretations just as vigorously as archaeologists debate how to interpret a site's stratigraphy or the distribution of artifacts in a surface scatter.

You'll be pleased to know that all four sets of standards make bows toward taking care of archaeological resources. Here, for example, is language from the "Rehabilitation" standards: "Archeological resources will be protected and preserved in place. If such resources must be disturbed, mitigation measures will be undertaken." Again, though, there's lots of room for interpretation, and it's not unheard of for people to honor this standard largely in the breach.

There's also a tricky issue in that adherence to the Standards can allow one to determine that a project will have *no adverse effect*, despite the fact that the disturbance of archaeological sites is obviously a form of destruction or alteration—both of which, by definition, are *adverse effects*. This matter tends to be winked at and ignored by historic preservation authorities, unless someone with a lot of political muscle makes trouble about it.

Practically speaking, if your project is going to have minor effects on archaeological stuff—say, disturbance of the kitchen midden associated with an old house in the course of doing foundation work on it—and you have a program in place to study the stuff in a responsible way, you're probably OK saying that there's no adverse effect. If you're going to do real damage to an archaeological site—or to anything else that anyone cares about—it's probably a lot wiser to acknowledge adverse effect and consult about ways to resolve it. Remember, there's nothing wrong with having an adverse effect.

The Third Example

"Removal of the property from its historic location" is an adverse effect—except when it's not. Where I grew up, there were a lot of small chicken houses (quite historic by now, in context) that were built on skids, making it easy to move them around. So, arguably, moving them wouldn't matter. And the warship on which I served in the Navy (doubtless historic and also scrapped by now) was by definition movable. But if the thing—usually a building or structure—wasn't meant to be moved, then moving it is an adverse effect, regardless of how justifiable such movement may be.

The Fourth Example

The fourth example is "change of the character of the property's use or of physical features within the property's setting that contribute to its historic significance." Say what?

OK, consider a place where people traditionally gather mushrooms. Suppose gathering mushrooms at this location is important to maintaining local traditions. If you make it infeasible to gather mushrooms there, you've changed the place's use, and that's an adverse effect.

Or suppose that looming over the mushroom field is a great huge rock. People who gather mushrooms there are always looking over their shoulders, worried about whether the rock will fall on them. Suppose you're going to dynamite the rock. Is that "chang[ing] the character of ... physical features within the property's setting that [maybe] contribute to its historical significance?"

Yes, if the rock contributes to the place's significance, and maybe it does. Maybe the very fact that 'shroom gatherers do their gathering in constant fear of getting squashed flat gives the place special cultural value; it's woven into the community's folklore. This doesn't mean the rock can't or shouldn't be dynamited—everyone might breathe a great sigh of relief if it is. But it's still an adverse effect that has to be acknowledged and discussed.

The Fifth Example

The fifth example is the "introduction of visual, atmospheric or audible elements that diminish the integrity of the property's significant historic features." Staying with our mushroom-gathering example, if you propose to build, say, a 30-meter high concrete mushroom 50 meters from the edge of the mushroom patch, does that introduce visual elements "that diminish the integrity" of the patch's "significant historic features?" If the thing is going to emit high-pitched screams when the wind is out of the southwest, is this an audible element that diminishes the patch's integrity? What if it attracts skunks?

Obviously, there's no simple or absolute answer. As usual, you will need to talk with the people who will be affected—the mushroom gatherers, and maybe those from elsewhere who attend the annual mushroom festival. And the mephitophobics.

The Sixth Example

The final example is "neglect of a property which causes its deterioration." This one can be tricky for several reasons.

First, you have to be in a position *to* neglect the place. I can't neglect your house; you can't neglect my apartment. So this example pretty much applies only to those who control land or buildings/structures. Plus, those in control have to be obligated to comply with the NHPA, or the example is irrelevant. So the example applies mostly to the actions/inactions of government agencies that manage land or maintain built things.

Second, you have to have the authority to take care of the place—to *not* neglect it. This is often an issue with privately owned facilities—mines, cabins, and the like—on government-controlled land. The government may not actually have the authority to care for the place if its owner decides to neglect it.

And, of course, taking care of a place usually costs money. Somebody's got to budget for it, and it may be that no one is in a position to do so. Or to do anything about someone's failure to do so.

So the neglect example tends to be a hard one to apply, and it often simply isn't applied. But it's there, and occasionally someone makes good use of it.

There's also a caveat—an exception—at the end of the example: "except where such neglect and deterioration are recognized qualities of a property of religious and cultural significance to an Indian tribe or Native Hawaiian organization." In other words, if a tribe or Native Hawaiian organization thinks it's quite all right for the building to fall down, for the site to erode, then letting it do so is *not* an adverse effect—provided that the significance of the place is "religious and cultural" in the eyes of the tribe or group. If the place's significance has other grounds to take into consideration—such as importance in archaeological research, or architectural value—then presumably the caveat doesn't apply. Or doesn't *entirely* apply. Or something. Yes, it's a mess.

Where Section 106 Does *Not* Apply

In countries other than the United States—that is, where Section 106 is not the law of the land—and in places *within* the United States where Section 106 isn't the law—that is, under state or local law—one doesn't have to fret about the criteria of adverse effect, either the main criterion or the examples. But in practical terms, you still have to figure out what effect, if any, the proposed action will have on whatever is culturally valued. Perhaps your government has its own criteria for judging adverse effect, and of course if it does, you have to address them. If it doesn't have such criteria, I don't think you'll go wrong by using the Section 106 criteria as a rough-and-ready guide, always understanding that you're not bound by their precise language.

Thinking back to the main criterion, for instance, ask this simple question of yourself and those with whom you're consulting: Is it likely that the project or activity will diminish the character of the place in a way that matters to people? Then apply the examples: Is it likely to destroy something that people care about? Is it likely to alter something in a way that people who value the place will find objectionable? Is it likely to change the environment in an objection-able way? What about its contribution to patterns of cumulative impact?

Thoughtfully applied, in consultation with all concerned, and without get-ting hung up on the fine points, the Section 106 criteria of adverse effect have broad utility. But of course there's a terrible human and institutional tendency to get hung up on the fine points.

What about Intangibles?

United States law and regulations are just as vague about how to address effects on "intangible" cultural resources as they are about identifying and evaluat-ing them. I think what's important to keep firmly in mind, however, is that there's often, maybe even usually, some kind of physical effect on physical stuff involved whenever you have impacts on something intangible. So there's usu-ally a basis for addressing effects on "intangibles" in Section 106 review.

After all, what is the "integrity" of a historic property, the thing whose diminution constitutes an adverse effect, if not the integrity of intangible con-ditions—of its perceived relationships with past events or patterns of events, of its "feeling," of its assumed information content? It's these elements of integrity we're supposed to be concerned about.

Several of the specific examples are also all about intangibles. The fourth example, change in character, is entirely an intangible matter. So is the fifth, pretty much—the introduction of incompatible elements. Then there's the second example: alteration is an adverse effect *unless* it's done in accordance with the Secretary's Standards, which are all about intangibilities such as archi-tectural style and authenticity.

There are changes to the environment that affect *only* intangible qualities—changes to, say, a system of education that subtly affects a community's attach-ment to its traditional language arts or the respect shown to elders by youth. These are tricky issues to address, and I don't know of anyone who's addressing them very well. Maybe UNESCO will show the way. I'd like to think so.

Avoiding an Adverse Effect Determination

There are often serious psychological, political, and economic pressures on a cli-ent or government agency to avoid acknowledging that effects will be adverse. Although there's no United States law that prohibits having adverse effects on historic places, it's generally understood to be undesirable. So for public rela-tions reasons, if nothing else, clients and agencies dislike admitting that they're going to damage historic places. You may find yourself under pressure not to use terminology that acknowledges adverse effect. You'll very likely be told that adverse effects can be made to go away if—well, if you can just talk about them in some other way. You may be told that they can be "mitigated away" (see below), although this usually requires that they first be acknowledged.

It's probably a fact that no one really *wants* to have adverse effects on valued cultural resources, or at least to be perceived as having them, so it's understandable that clients and employers want you to avoid acknowledging that they will occur. But the law—United States law, at least—doesn't require that adverse effects be avoided; it doesn't even discourage agencies of government from having them. It simply requires that they be "taken into account." Taking adverse effects into account, the regulations make clear, simply means trying to figure out how to avoid, reduce, or otherwise "mitigate" them, and trying to reach agreement on a strategy for doing so.

Figuring Out What to Do about It

Under the NHPA Section 106 regulations, the responsible federal agency applies the criteria of adverse effect, in consultation with the SHPO, THPO, and (hopefully, although the regulations are not very explicit about it) other interested parties. If they decide that the criteria are met, then that means there will be an adverse effect, and the next step is to figure out what—if anything— to do about it. While the systems employed by other governments differ from those employed in the United States, one way or another, everyone winds up confronted with this essential question. Carrying out something that a government wants to do—or that it's being asked to approve by issuing a permit or providing financial assistance—will have adverse effects on some set of cultural resources, tangible and/or intangible. How do we decide what to do about it?

Study Questions

1. Thinking of a project that's known to you (perhaps from one of the preceding chapters), or making one up, and assuming that one or more cultural resources are in its vicinity, what might you conclude about the project's potential effects based on applying the Section 106 criteria of adverse effect?
2. Suppose you see that an adverse effect will occur, but your client really doesn't want to acknowledge it. What do you say and do?
3. Suppose an archaeological site is going to be destroyed by a project, but nobody involved—client, regulators, local people—cares about it. Is there anything you can do? *Should* do?

Further Reading

Criteria of Adverse Effect, etc.

Advisory Council on Historic Preservation (ACHP). 2004. Protection of Historic
    Properties, 36 CFR Part 800. http://www.achp.gov/regs-rev04.pdf.
    These are the United States government regulations governing the review of
    project effects on historic properties (not all cultural resources). Section 800.5
    deals with assessing whether effects are adverse, and includes the criteria of
    adverse effect.

ACHP. n.d. *Questions and Answers about the Criteria of Adverse Effect.* http://www.
    achp.gov/106q&a.html#800.5.
    Not very helpful, to my mind, but they're what we've been given.

King, Thomas F. 2003. *Places That Count: Traditional Cultural Properties in Cultural
    Resource Management.* Lanham, MD: Altamira Press.
    My textbook on traditional cultural places (TCPs) in general. Chapter 9 is
    about interpreting the ACHP criteria of adverse effect with respect to TCPs.

United States Secretary of the Interior. n.d. *Standards for the Treatment of Historic
    Properties: 36 CFR Part 68.* https://www.nps.gov/tps/standards.htm.
    These "Secretary's Standards" are referenced in the ACHP criteria of adverse
    effect.

Chapter 5

What CRM Archaeologists Do
Resolving Adverse Effects

———m———

To Mitigate or Not to Mitigate: That Is the Question

Some archaeologists seem to think that if there's going to be an adverse effect, the law requires that it be "mitigated"—that one moves seamlessly from impact assessment to "mitigation." In the United States at least, that's not exactly true, and I doubt if it's true anywhere.

Merriam-Webster Online tells us that "to mitigate" means "to cause to become less harsh or hostile," or "to make less severe or painful." Synonyms include "to mollify" and "to alleviate." The regulations of the United States Council on Environmental Quality (CEQ) for implementing the procedural aspects of the NEPA include a helpfully simple and inclusive definition. They say that impact "mitigation" includes:

(a) Avoiding the impact altogether by not taking a certain action or parts of an action.
(b) Minimizing impacts by limiting the degree or magnitude of the action and its implementation.
(c) Rectifying the impact by repairing, rehabilitating, or restoring the affected environment.
(d) Reducing or eliminating the impact over time by preservation and maintenance operations during the life of the action.
(e) Compensating for the impact by replacing or providing substitute resources or environments.

In the United States, with respect to those cultural resources definable as "historic properties," we use the NHPA Section 106 process to establish what sort of mitigation—if any—will be carried out. We consult, that is, negotiate, about ways to make the damage less harsh, less severe, about ways to alleviate it, about how to make that alleviation happen. We look at options, including those that make the adverse effect go away altogether, those that compensate for it in some manner, and those that fall in between these extremes.

Archaeologists, however, often understand "mitigation" to mean something more specific—something that's often not satisfactory from the standpoint of those who want to preserve a place, and that can be costly to those who *don't* want to preserve it. I heard recently about a Native American elder who said that his language includes no word for "mitigation." I suspect he's mistaken; it would be a cruel language that didn't include terms for "causing to become less harsh and hostile," or "causing to become less severe and painful." I suspect that what he meant was: "My language has no word for digging up the remains of the ancestors and thus making everything OK."

Digging up—doing salvage or rescue archaeology—has come to be widely equated with "mitigation" in the minds of indigenous people and archaeologists alike, though it's not what the word means. Impact mitigation *can* entail doing archaeological excavation *if* it's agreed that doing so will cause effects to become less harsh and hostile, less severe and painful. But it is by no means the standard thing to do that some archaeologists, and some descendant communities, think it is.

And while the NHPA Section 106 regulations (which don't define "mitigation," by the way) provide for us to negotiate ways to resolve adverse effects, they don't require that we *succeed.* Often enough we fail. At that point, a bullet has to be bitten. Will we go ahead and do the damage without alleviation, without making it less harsh, less painful? Or will we say, "The damage would be too great," and abandon the damaging action?

I've seen both things happen, but in most cases people agree on some form of mitigation.

"Resolving" Adverse Effects

To summarize: once we've established that adverse effects will likely occur, we try to figure out a way to make them less harsh and hostile, less severe and painful—in other words, to mitigate them. We do this by placing *alternatives* on the table and seeing what our consulting partners think of them.

The Section 106 regulations refer to these alternatives as potential means of "resolving" adverse effects. Confusingly, they say that resolution of an adverse effect may involve its "avoidance" *or* its "minimization" *or* its "mitigation"—as though avoiding or minimizing adverse effects does not make those effects less harsh, hostile, severe, or painful, and as though the NEPA regulations didn't define "mitigation" to *include* avoidance and minimization.

Section 106 literalists—who abound in the business and invariably ignore both the dictionary and the NEPA regulations—often conclude that the placement of these three words in sequence means that avoidance must be preferred to minimization, which must in turn be given priority over mitigation. This is nonsense. In any human language, words are necessarily laid out in sequence; you can't pile them up on top of each other and communicate anything. So of course, once the regulation writers decided to use the words "avoidance," "minimization," and "mitigation," they put them in sequence. This no more implies a priority order than listing, say, "cats, dogs, and elephants" would mean that cats should be chosen over dogs, who in turn are preferable to pachyderms. And just as some families may like to have both cats and dogs in their homes, and to visit elephants at the zoo, it's not uncommon to resolve adverse effects by avoiding some of them, minimizing others, and finding other ways to mitigate others.

I say "other ways" because the dictionary implies and the NEPA regulations specify that avoiding and minimizing adverse effects are *ways* to mitigate them. So maybe my analogy should be to a list including "cats, dogs, or mammals"—which wouldn't make any sense, but neither does "avoid, minimize, or mitigate." People get into horrible, time-wasting arguments about abstractions like word sequence. I strongly advise that you try to avoid them.

The bottom line is simply this: having recognized that adverse effects are likely to occur, the responsible agency is supposed to consult—with the relevant regulatory bodies and whoever's likely to be affected by the proposed action—about what can be done to make the effects less adverse. It's really no more complicated than that. We often *make* it more complicated, but that's our choice. There's nothing in the law or regulations—in the United States, at least—that requires us to complicate the process.

Who's Responsible?

So who consults to resolve adverse effects? Who's responsible for it? In the United States under Section 106 of the NHPA, it's whatever federal agency has to make a go/no-go decision about a proposed project or other action. But the agency can and often does delegate a major role in handling consultation to the (usually non-federal) project proponent.

The proponent obviously has a big stake in having the consultation work out in its favor, so placing the proponent in charge can amount to handing the henhouse keys to the fox. It's generally wiser to have a (theoretically) objective government agency in charge, drawing liberally on the expertise of the project proponent but not trusting its experts too much. Unfortunately, a lot of agencies are very, very trusting—and lack the staff and resources to be otherwise. This is an ongoing problem with all kinds of EIA work; it needs serious attention but is unlikely to get it in the immediate future.

If worse comes to worst and the proponent seems to have too heavy a thumb on the scale, another party in the consultation can appeal the matter up the chain of command of the (theoretically) responsible agency, and/or to the SHPO and/or ACHP. Or go public in the media. Sometimes these strategies work; sometimes they don't.

If you're operating under some authority other than Section 106 of the NHPA, then who's responsible for consultation—if anyone—depends on what the relevant laws and regulations say. Generally, though, some government agency will have the job of organizing and overseeing whatever is done.

Who Gets Consulted?

Depending on the legal authority, certain parties may *have* to be consulted. Under Section 106 of the NHPA, the SHPO or (on tribal lands) THPO is always at the table. Maybe a local government, too; maybe a state agency, occasionally the ACHP, sometimes the National Trust for Historic Preservation, in special cases the National Park Service. Perhaps an Indian tribe, Alaska Native Group, or Native Hawaiian organization, particularly if they have cultural associations with the place(s) subject to adverse effect.

The people who most need to be consulted, though, are not always those listed in government regulations. I'm talking, of course, about people whose cultural heritage—or other interests—may be affected by the proposed action. These are the people with whom I work these days. Some of my current and recent clients are Indian tribes in Washington State, Alaska, and Oklahoma, private property owners in Virginia, Maryland and Oregon, and families in Louisiana who were displaced from their farms by the United States Army during World War II. Several things make it complicated for people like these to participate in consultation.

- First, they're usually not environmental or heritage lawyers, and often don't know how the relevant laws work or what rights those laws afford them.
- Second, they often don't have much money, so it's hard—even impossible—for them to pay for specialist lawyers and "experts" like me (yes, I do a lot of work for free, but there's a limit).
- Third, they usually have to work at 9-to-5 jobs, and it's hard for them to take time off for meetings, field trips, and the like.
- Fourth, they don't know the bureaucratic lingo, and it's relatively easy for them to be snowed.
- Fifth, their concerns often don't fall easily into standard "historic preservation" categories. One of my clients is mostly concerned about salmon; another cares strongly about wild horses; another is seriously focused on trees. Another is devoted to preserving the brick streets laid down by African-American ancestors in one of the country's first "free Black" communities. Another wants to save dugongs from the United States Navy.

It may take some serious discussion and wordsmithing to persuade the Powers That Be that these are real cultural resource, heritage, historic preservation concerns, but they sure as hell are to the people who hold them, and those people ought to have seats at the consultation table. But they often don't get there without a fight—if they get there at all.

The Process of Consultation

Your agency or client should have been consulting—deliberating together, remember?—from the very start. Consulting about the APE and the scope of identification work. Consulting about the significance of what's been found and how it may be affected. But now you're coming to the crux of things—what's going to be *done*. We discussed this in chapter 2, but I think it's worth reminding ourselves that, according to the NHPA Section 106 regulations at 36 CFR 800.16(f), "consultation" means "the process of *seeking, discussing,* and *considering* the views of other participants, and, where feasible, *seeking agreement* with them regarding matters arising in the section 106 process" (emphasis added).

The regulations, recall, go on to refer to the "Secretary of the Interior's Standards and Guidelines for Federal Agency Historic Preservation Programs Pursuant to the National Historic Preservation Act" for further guidance. These are different from the "Secretary of the Interior's Standards for the Treatment of Historic Properties" just discussed in such tedious detail; I'm sorry.

Among much else, remember, *these* "Standards and Guidelines" say that whoever's responsible for the consultation should:

1. Make its interests and constraints clear at the beginning;
2. Make clear any rules, processes, or schedules applicable to the consultation;
3. Acknowledge others' interests as legitimate, and seek to understand them;
4. Develop and consider a full range of options; and,
5. Try to identify solutions that will leave all parties satisfied.

Importantly, they point out that "although time limits may be necessary on specific transactions carried out in the course of consultation (e.g., the time allowed to respond to an inquiry), there should be no hard-and-fast time limit on consultation overall. *Consultation on a specific undertaking should proceed until agreement is reached or until it becomes clear that agreement cannot be reached*" (emphasis added).

There are two options: (1) agreement, and (2) realization that agreement isn't going to happen. This is pretty straightforward, but the parties who are trying to reach agreement may have quite dramatically different ideas about what's agreeable.

The project proponent presumably wants more than anything else to get the project completed, as quickly and inexpensively as possible. A preservation organization may want the historic character of the community protected above all else. An indigenous group may want to protect the remains of its ancestors, or the integrity of the environment to which its members ascribe spiritual significance. These may be utterly incompatible objectives.

Or they may not. Finding out what's incompatible and what's not, looking for common ground—that's what consultation should be about.

Depending on your job assignment and your status in the organization, you may or may not have much to do with how consultation is structured, but if you can, try to get the issues framed broadly, flexibly.

Some of your colleagues are likely to want to frame those issues very narrowly, saying, for example, that X, Y, or Z (e.g., involving salmon, horses, or dugongs) is not "a cultural resource issue," or is "not within the scope of Section 106" (or whatever legal authority applies). Often this kind of stuff comes from the project proponent's lawyers, but often enough you'll hear it from the SHPO or some other "cultural resource expert." They may technically be right (though they're probably not), but right or wrong, they're being thickheaded. You don't reach agreement with people if you start the discussion by telling them their concerns are off the table.

Whether the law precisely requires it or not, you're better off if people feel that they've been respectfully involved in decision making, rather than that they've been excluded. Virtually every revolution in world history illustrates this principle. So my recommendation is to try to get everybody to the table—even if that requires driving or flying them there, putting them up in hotels, covering the cost of their meals. And don't for a moment let anyone imply that their agreement is being *bought*. It's a tricky line to walk, but it can be done. I'm not very good at it, but I've seen people do it magnificently.

There will be a tendency at any consultation meeting for the agency in charge to try to manage things according to its own standard operating procedures. That's fine up to a point; there are reasons why standard operating procedures have become standard. But be careful! It's often the case that standard operating procedures have evolved—often without anyone's deliberate intent— to exclude from participation the very people who most need to participate.

It's common, for example, for a meeting to give pride of place to elected officials and their representatives. "We will now hear from the representative of Senator Suchandso." Who may have nothing but platitudes to offer. Get too many of these, and the people most concerned—the property owners, the local heritage group, the indigenous community—are dozing off in the back of the room. Or getting more and more pissed off, while running out of time to make their concerns known.

It's hard, but it'll help everyone—including the project proponent—if you can cut through the rigmarole and get everybody to the point. The point being:

1. What's proposed?
2. What adverse effects may it have?
3. What alternatives have been considered?
4. What alternatives *ought* to be considered?
5. What are the ways we can consider them?

It may be—I've seen this happen—that you get to item 3, and the project's opponents say, "Well, OK, if you tweak Alternative 7b a little bit, we'll be fine."

Or you get to item 4, and the proponent says, "Oh, you want us to do X? We can do that." If such a thing happens, you want to capture the agreement quickly in some form of documentation—typically, a Memorandum of Agreement (MOA) in the NHPA Section 106 process. There's lots of guidance about how to write such things (see "Documenting Agreement" below).[1]

Of course, you can't count on such a happy result—particularly not in a single meeting. Consultation almost always involves multiple meetings, in multiple venues. Claudia Nissley and I have written about this in our 2014 book, *Consultation and Cultural Heritage*, and there's plenty of general guidance in famous books like *Getting to Yes* and *Getting Past No*—as well as less famous ones like *Negotiating Across Cultures*—all listed under "Further Reading" below and highly recommended. There are also classes in consultation—under various names—offered by the United States Institute for Environmental Conflict Resolution and others.

There may be considerable disagreement about item 2—what adverse effects may the action have? How a given party responds is likely to depend on how that party relates to the effects, and this is often where archaeology becomes an issue. The project proponent, the overseeing agency, and maybe a regulatory agency or two are likely to want to define impacts very narrowly, pragmatically, and those pragmatic definitions often are archaeological. Yes, we're going to bulldoze out Archaeological Site XB72, but, hey, it's no big deal. We'll have our archaeologists dig everything up in advance, and all will be well.

This may seem sensible to those who propose it, but if Site XB72 is the ancestral home of the Veryold Tribe (or Native Group or First Nation), the members of that Tribe, Group, or Nation may not be at all pleased with the idea of digging everything up—or even with referring to the place as an "archaeological site" and giving it a number. Somebody needs to find out what—if anything— *will* please them. This may require the deployment of some non-archaeological but very anthropological sensitivities and skills.

Exactly what's involved in reaching agreement depends on the case, the issues, the parties in negotiation, and the legal regime under which the consultation takes place. In this short book I couldn't begin to outline all the possibilities, even if I knew them all. It can be an exciting, rewarding experience to help disparate parties "get to yes," and every case is a new challenge.

Unfortunately, there's a very strong motivation on the part of project proponents and oversight agencies to short-circuit consultation, to get the damn thing done so we can move on to other stuff—other things piling up on our desks, other things we're more interested in. This can result in agreements that exclude key parties and ignore important effects.

The Kick-the-Can Syndrome

The urge to reach an agreement, regardless of its utility, often leads to agreements-to-agree, that is, to kick the can of mitigation decision making down the road. Usually couched in obscure terms, laden with verbiage, such a kick-the-can setup outlines a program not only of *mitigation*, but also of *identification* and *effect determination* that will be carried out *after* a project is approved. Such an approach can be useful, and sometimes it's necessary, but it can also create needless complications, frustrate public participation, and thwart the expressed will of Congress—which was, after all, that effects on historic places be taken into account *before* decisions are made that may affect them.

I can't begin to go into all the pros and cons of can-kicking in this short book, but just suppose, for example, that you're a federal agency and you're asked to approve or assist in building a bridge across an inlet of the sea between an urbanized area and one that's pretty rural. The potential effects of this undertaking are extensive and complicated, but predictable. Besides its direct impacts (physical, visual, auditory, etc.), it will allow traffic to cross the inlet and almost certainly spur new development on its rural shore and beyond. If you're doing Section 106 review honestly and honorably, then *prior* to making a decision about building the bridge, you'll take these potential effects into account by doing what the regulations tell you to do. You'll consult, you'll establish an APE that embraces all the potential direct, indirect, and cumulative effects, you'll carry out a reasonable program of identification and effect determination, and you'll try to negotiate an agreement about how to mitigate the adverse effects you'll almost certainly find.

But that's a lot of trouble, and it's made more troublesome by people's groundless but often firmly held belief that it's necessary to describe and evaluate painstakingly every site, building, structure, and object before you can consider effects on them. So you may be very tempted—and advised by professional consultants, by the SHPO, and even by the ACHP—to put off all that trouble until *after* you decide to help build the bridge, and even until after you decide where and how it will be built. *Then* you'll do what the regulations say to do. But then it will be too late to influence decision making.

Of course, this stands the straightforward language of Congress precisely on its head, so I strongly advise that you not do it, but you're very likely to be told by SHPOs, the ACHP, and other official experts that kick-the-can agreements are just fine. They're not. Sometimes they're necessary, strategically or politically or just pragmatically, but as a rule, we ought to try to achieve agreements about impact mitigation that actually describe how impacts will be mitigated.

Documenting Agreement

Depending on the legal system under which you're working, and the political power of the parties involved, you may or may not need to get *everyone* involved to agree on a means of resolving adverse effect, but obviously the more parties you have on board, the better. In the United States under Section 106 of the NHPA, you typically need the agreement of the responsible federal agency and the relevant SHPO or THPO. Tribes have to agree to actions taking place on lands under their control (or held in trust for them), and local governments may have their own independent sources of authority that make it near-mandatory to have their agreement. Ironically, non-governmental project proponents technically don't need to agree because the federal agency on whose permit or assistance they depend can force them to go along. But nobody likes to talk about that, and in point of fact it's not very practical. It's preferable to have the project proponent agree.

Other parties in the United States—often including those most affected, like tribes on non-tribal lands, tribes that aren't recognized by the federal government, property owners, and citizens' groups—*don't* have to agree. They have to be consulted, presumably listened to, perhaps reasoned with. But when push comes to shove, if they don't agree, the other consulting parties can execute the paperwork (see below) and have a binding agreement. Is this right? Is it democratic? Honorable people can disagree. But it's the way it is.

Be this as it may, it's a really good idea to try to get everyone on board with the agreement. And whether or not you're successful, it's important to maintain a detailed record of your negotiations. What has each party said? What has each party sought in the negotiations? What interests, grievances, and concerns has each party brought to the table? How have all these been addressed? Which issues have been resolved and which have not? Why and why not?

I hasten to say that I've never been good at keeping all those records, though I think I'm fairly able to keep everyone's arguments in my head until a meeting is over and I can get to my keyboard and try to make sense of it all. Others I know are really good at keeping notes. This is a tremendously useful skill, and I recommend that you try to attain it. A lot of the student-oriented advice on the website https://www.wikihow.com/Take-Better-Notes is relevant, and will serve you well in your CRM career. I wish I'd had it to follow.

Memoranda of Agreement and Their Kin

Assuming you *do* reach agreement among the parties, you need to document it in some way. Under Section 106 of the NHPA, agreement is usually documented in a Memorandum of Agreement (MOA). If you've managed to reach an agreement that utterly avoids adverse effect—that is, gets you to the point where the criteria of adverse effect *aren't* met—then you can document this with an exchange of letters. But that's messy, so my recommendation is to memorialize the agreement in an MOA. My somewhat antiquated book, *Federal Planning and Historic Places*, goes into detail about writing an MOA, and the ACHP and National Preservation Institute (NPI) provide guidance on their websites. Claudia Nissley and I discuss the art of MOA writing in *Consultation and Cultural Heritage*.

I'll just offer a few suggestions here, but they're *very strong suggestions*. I think it's little short of tragic how the art of agreement drafting has deteriorated in the last 20 years of practice under Section 106. Neither the ACHP nor the SHPOs seem much to care anymore, resulting in a lot of MOAs and other agreements that are almost impossible to understand—or, worse, that can be understood in all sorts of different ways. Such an agreement is worse than useless; it undercuts the whole purpose of CRM consultation.

To avoid such an outcome, I recommend the following:

- Begin with an outline of what's agreed to. Make sure you and everyone else understand what that *is*. Put it in simple language. "No digging within 50 meters of the Giant Oak." "Demolish the east wing of the Old Main Dormitory." "Run the power line along the south side of Highway 601."
- Emphasize the main, substantive points—*then* think and write about the administrivia necessary to bring the main points to fruition.
- Look at old models—agreements similar to yours that others have composed—but *don't parrot them!* Think about whether and how their terms are and are not applicable to your situation, and modify them as needed. Don't be afraid to make up *altogether new* stipulations, new language. Don't let your computer's hard drive substitute for your brain![2]

Drafting an agreement—like negotiating one—can be fun and intellectually stimulating, or it can be drudgework. If it becomes the latter, that may be a warning that you're messing up.

About Archaeology

If the consulting parties have agreed on archaeological research as all or part of the impact mitigation package, you need to be careful about how such research is stipulated. It's easy to say, "Site 799 will be subjected to archaeological data recovery," but you need to go beyond that. How will the work be done? What research questions will be addressed? How will they be addressed? How will results be analyzed and recorded and reported to the world? How will recovered materials be cared for, managed, preserved, analyzed? What will be returned to descendant communities, or to the ground? How will the interested public be involved? How will arguments over all these issues be resolved? And of course, who will pay for it all, and how? All these questions should be answered somewhere, and that somewhere—a research design, a data recovery plan, whatever it's called—should be referenced in the MOA. If it's going to take some time to implement the work, the MOA should provide for revisions, updates, and adaptation to changing circumstances.

Someone in your food chain may puff out his chest and say, "We don't use the word 'research' for the archaeology we have to do." That's nonsense; ignore it. If your clients are going to mess up an archaeological site, the least they can do is conduct the research necessary to record what the place was like and the contributions it made to the world's corpus of historical, anthropological, and other knowledge. What's done ought to be *good* research, *productive* research that teaches the world something useful about the past, and maybe about the present and future.

I also need to highlight the importance of being specific—as mentioned fleetingly above—about how the data and materials produced by the work will be cared for, managed, preserved, and made available to scholarship and the public. All that is (often) collectively referred to as "curation." Curation is a considerable responsibility, and one you need to reflect on carefully. How are the products of the work you're calling for—the artifacts, the ecofacts, the samples, the field notes, the photographs, the digital records—going to be taken care of? You need to think about this, consult about this, and come up with a plan before you start digging or otherwise producing data. The plan should be referenced in the MOA.

You may need to provide for *repatriation*—returning artifacts, human remains, and other cultural items to descendant communities, including communities that you may not readily acknowledge as descendant. In the United States this is pretty uniformly required for Native American remains under the Native American Graves Protection and Repatriation Act (NAGPRA). Even if it's not legally required, it may be what's agreed to. You may not like it—I have misgivings about repatriation, for what little that's worth—but on the whole I think it's the right thing to do, if people desire it. And in any event, it may be what's agreed to, so whether you or I think it's a good idea is rather beside the point.

Beyond Archaeology

But I don't want to imply that archaeological research is all an MOA can or should provide for. Commonly, MOAs provide for the following sorts of things, among many others:

- Adoption of a project alternative that avoids or minimizes damage: putting the pipeline down *that* valley rather than *this* one; limiting the height of the building; orienting the airport in *that* direction rather than *this* one; removing Building X from the project plans.
- Rehabilitation and adaptive use of historic buildings, structures, and designed landscapes—usually but *not necessarily* following the Secretary of the Interior's Standards. If the responsible agency wants to demonstrate that its project will have "no adverse effect" based on *adherence* to the Standards, then obviously they *do* have to be followed. But if you're writing an MOA, adverse effect has been acknowledged, so you have more latitude.
- Landscaping to minimize visual, auditory, and other impacts, such as plantings to screen ugly stuff, noise barriers, or planting sweet-smelling plants to mask nasty odors.
- Implementation of management plans. Be careful of this one; it's often a way to kick the can down the road, but in some cases, such plans can be helpful.
- Preservation, rehabilitation, and ongoing management of sites, structures, buildings, and landscapes to compensate for things destroyed or damaged.

"We'll knock down Building X, but acquire, rehabilitate, and reuse Buildings Y and Z."

- Creation and management of funds to support such compensatory activities.
- Architectural, engineering, and landscape documentation.
- Creation of museums, exhibits, books, videos, and other interpretative facilities.
- And pretty much anything else that's imaginable and legal.

Writing a good agreement is something of an art form, and if you can learn to do it well, it may help convince people that they should hire and retain you. For that matter, being able to write *anything* well can give you a leg up in CRM. Keeping good fieldnotes, keeping good notes on meetings, keeping track of consulting parties, and writing agreements that clearly, concisely, and accurately capture what's been agreed to—all these skills will improve your employment prospects.

What If There's Nothing to Do about It?

But what if you *can't* reach agreement on some means of mitigating adverse effects? Or what if you couldn't do anything reasonable even if you *did* reach agreement? What if the effects are just too adverse?

Under the NHPA Section 106 regulations, if agreement can't be reached, the responsible federal agency seeks a final, formal comment from the ACHP. This comment—the ACHP's recommendation—goes to the relevant agency's top dog, the cabinet secretary or equivalent who oversees the agency. The law requires that top dog to chew on it—give the matter her or his personal consideration—and then make a public decision. But there's no constraint on what the decision can be.

The top dog, in the end, can piddle on the project, or pee on preservation. Or squat somewhere between the two. To my cynical readers who I imagine are saying, "Oh sure, so in the end the project proponents always get their way," I can respond that this has been my experience in only about 50 percent of the "no agreement" cases with which I've been involved. I recommend to my non-agency clients that they not be too willing to sign an MOA. In the end, it may be a better strategy to refuse to agree and put the agency in a position where it has to go on record as saying, in essence, "Screw you." Agencies don't like to do that. Or rather, they may be perfectly happy to *do it*—to screw the public and the environment—but they don't like to *acknowledge* doing it. Acknowledgment can have political consequences.

But look, you're unlikely to get involved in a "no agreement" situation, at least until you've gained enough experience to make this book no longer useful to you, so we don't need to belabor the point. I just want to be clear about the fact that *agreement is not required*. In the final analysis, the legal requirement in the United States is for the ACHP to comment and the agency to pay attention—but not necessarily do what the ACHP says.

And there's no requirement that the ACHP come down on the side of preservation; it can tell the agency to crank up the 'dozers, swing the wrecking ball, and get on with it. I've never seen that happen, however. Even in the most development-happy administrations, the ACHP has tended to favor preservation. So far.

As to other countries, as usual I'm ill-informed, but my marginal acquaintance with a few nasty cases in Latin America, Australia, Europe, and Canada suggests to me that "no agreement" cases move rather rapidly into the political and legal arenas. You're trying to influence Parliament or making a case in court, or taking to the streets.

Study Questions

1. Give five examples of impact mitigation.
2. Someone says, "The Section 106 regulations don't allow us to discuss mitigation until you've demonstrated that avoidance is not feasible." How do you respond?
3. Who do you think it is most important to consult when exploring ways to mitigate a proposed project's adverse effects? Why?
4. Take a look at the MOA guidance at https://www.achp.gov/initiatives/guidance-agreement-documents. What do you think of it?

Notes

1. Variants on the MOA theme include "programmatic agreements" (PAs) and "program comments" (PCs)—agreements in effect covering whole agency programs or really large, usually ill-defined projects.
2. A hat tip to Claudia Nissley for contributions to this rant.

Further Reading

(See previous chapter readings with regard to laws, consultation, etc.)

Cohen, Raymond. (1991) 2002. *Negotiating Across Cultures: International Communication in an Interdependent World*. Rev. ed. Washington, DC: United States Institute of Peace Press.
> Cohen focuses on the complexities and pitfalls of negotiating—that is, consulting, between nations with diverse cultural backgrounds. His observations are very relevant to work with Indian tribes and other indigenous communities, though these are not his focus.

Dorochoff, Nicholas. 2007. *Negotiation Basics for Cultural Resource Managers*. New York: Routledge.
> A hands-on guide to negotiating in the course of NHPA Section 106 and similar consultations.

Fisher, Roger, and William Ury. 1981. *Getting to Yes: Negotiating Agreement without Giving In*. New York: Houghton Mifflin.
> This is the granddaddy of books on consultation-to-agreement. Though criticized by some (like Cohen) for having a culturally limited perspective, it's loaded with useful guidelines, and is essential reading.

King, Thomas F. 2000. *Federal Planning and Historic Places*. Lanham, MD: Altamira Press.
> My rather dated treatment of the NHPA Section 106 process; devotes a good deal of space to the fine points of writing an MOA

Nissley, Claudia, and Thomas F. King. 2014. *Consultation and Cultural Heritage: Let Us Reason Together*. New York: Routledge.
> Our effort to outline principles and best practices of consultation on cultural heritage/resource matters.

United States National Park Service. n.d. "National NAGPRA." https://www.nps.gov/nagpra/mandates/index.htm.
> The Native American Graves Protection and Repatriation Act (NAGPRA) must often be complied with when resolving adverse effects on historic properties. This site provides guidance about how to comply.

United States Secretary of the Interior. n.d. "Secretary of Interior's Standards and Guidelines for Federal Agency Historic Preservation Programs Pursuant to the National Historic Preservation Act." https://www.energy.gov/nepa/downloads/secretary-interiors-standards-and-guidelines-federal-agency-historic-preservation.
> These "Standards and Guidelines" include advice about consultation regarding things like the resolution of adverse effect.

Ury, William. 1991. *Getting Past No: Negotiating in Difficult Situations*. New York: Bantam Books.
> Ury's sequel to his and Fisher's *Getting to Yes*, based on years of hard-won experience in cases where "yes" was not easily obtainable.

Chapter 6

What Else Do CRM Archaeologists Do?

So far, we've focused mostly on what CRM archaeologists do in environmental impact assessment (EIA) under legal systems like those prescribed in the United States by the NEPA and Section 106 of the NHPA. EIA is the biggest driver of CRM in the United States, but there are other ways that CRM is done and other things that CRM archaeologists do. Some of these ways and things, I think, pass muster a lot better than do others as *management* of *cultural resources*, but the term is routinely applied to them, or CRM archaeologists routinely find themselves wrapped up in them, so we need to address them. In this chapter we'll touch on land and building management, the acquisition and conduct of studies, construction monitoring, and keeping things secret.

Land and Building Management

You may find yourself employed by a land management agency. In the United States, the biggies are the Bureau of Land Management (BLM), Fish and Wildlife Service (FWS), and National Park Service (NPS) in the Department of the Interior (DOI); the Forest Service in the Department of Agriculture (USDA); the Army, Navy, and Air Force in the Department of Defense (DOD); the Department of Energy (DOE); and the Department of Veterans Affairs (VA). Or you may find employment in an agency that manages a lot of buildings, like the General Services Administration (GSA), or, again, the DOD and VA. Since the September 11 attacks in 2001, several agencies have coagulated under the aegis of the Department of Homeland Security (DHS), some of which—like the Coast Guard and the Border Patrol—manage land and/or buildings.

In an agency that manages land or buildings, you'll be involved in NHPA Section 106 review whenever something is proposed—by your agency or somebody else—that may affect what your agency manages. This is assuming your agency complies with the law—a less than safe bet, especially where the DHS is concerned. But beyond managing Section 106 cases, you may have other obligations and opportunities.

For example, there's Section 110 of the NHPA. In the interests of full disclosure, I worked on major amendments to Section 110 enacted by Congress in 1992, and on the Department of the Interior's guidelines for its implementation. Section 110 was an attempt to establish agency responsibilities that go beyond "taking into account" the effects of undertakings, as provided for by Section 106, and to put agency Section 106 responsibilities in some sort of logical context. It essentially requires agency heads to be responsible for historic properties that are under their control or are subject to effect by their decisions, and lays out several more or less specific ways this responsibility is supposed to be exercised.

To me, the most important Section 110 requirements are those that undergird and elaborate on Section 106 responsibilities, including the responsibility to consult with stakeholders. But the one that gets the most attention is the requirement, quoting the NPS website, to "establish a preservation program for the identification, evaluation, nomination to the National Register, and protection of historic properties."

This is a widely misunderstood requirement, and in retrospect rather poorly written (the product of a rump committee[1] on which I served). But it's not inaccurately understood to mean that each agency should try to figure out what historic properties (a *subset* of "cultural resources," remember) it's responsible for managing, and to manage them in a "protective" way. Though technically applicable to all agencies, it mostly affects those that manage land or buildings.

Most agency Section 110 programs I know of have focused mainly on figuring out what they have to manage, and this has led them to conduct surveys, including background studies, and to nominate places to the NRHP. If you work for a land or building management agency, you'll likely have oversight of such work as part of your job description. This can be pretty neat; it can give you the time and money to do, or contract with others to do, research that *you* think is interesting. But you need to be responsible about it.

Think about your agency's management needs. Maybe *you'd* really like to know about Pleistocene hunting patterns, but there's not a whole lot likely to happen to Pleistocene hunting campsites on the lands your agency manages. However, there may be big issues surrounding privately owned fishing piers: conservationists may want them removed, while their owners may say, "Hell, no!" Your agency may need to know which piers are eligible for the NRHP and engage the various parties in consultation, a helluva lot more urgently than it needs to learn about Pleistocene hunting camps.

Doing Studies

The standard agency response to Section 110 is to fund *studies* comprising background research and field surveys, often leading to NRHP nominations. The NPS encourages this; it regards nominations as "good things to do," whether they're useful for anything or not. Similar studies are often done under Section 106 as well, either to assess the potential impacts of a proposed action or (ostensibly) to mitigate an action's adverse effects.

Of What, and How?

If you find yourself tempted or encouraged to get your agency to sponsor a study, I suggest that you ask yourself this simple question: What do we need to know in order to manage the historic stuff we (knowingly or not) manage or affect? Pleistocene hunting camps or fishing piers? Battlefields or garages? Places in the RunningRiver watershed, or the main buildings on all our installations? By "we," of course, I mean your agency and the public it serves. And do you necessarily need to nominate anything to the NRHP? Nomination is costly, time-consuming, and often not very relevant to management. You may be able to get along very well with some simpler way of describing what you identify.

It may be that what would best serve the public and your agency isn't a survey at all—whether of hunting camps or fishing piers or battlefields or garages. Maybe what's needed—and perfectly appropriate under the authority of NHPA Section 110—is to study a *problem*, an *issue*, an *opportunity.* What's happening with coastal erosion on lands under your agency's jurisdiction, and how may this be affecting cultural resources? Are there plants or animals that contribute to the character of cultural places and that are in trouble? Do local communities have all the opportunities they need or want to carry out cultural activities on the agency's land? Are there conflicts between such activities and the agency's missions? If so, how can these be resolved? Are there channels for cooperation between the agency and local communities or other interest groups?

So you establish what's needed—in consultation with others inside and outside the agency, to the extent that it's feasible. Then, of course, you need to figure out *how to do what's needed* (in consultation, I hope, with others). What's the scope of work? What's the budget? These can be very creative enterprises, though your agency will probably have guidelines for you to follow. These should be attended to—they're usually based on substantial, if not always relevant, experience—but they shouldn't be taken as Holy Writ. Try to figure out what's really needed, and what it realistically may cost.

The Request for Proposals

It's very unlikely that you'll perform the study yourself; 99 times out of 100 your agency will contract for it. You'll work with your contracting people to turn your thinking into a request for proposals (RFP), which your agency will publish, inviting people and institutions to propose how they'll do the work you need done.

If you can, try to avoid letting your contracting people—or your agency's lawyers—completely control the RFP development process. Contracting people have definite ideas about how an RFP ought to look; many of these are grounded in the Federal Acquisition Regulation (FAR) or its equivalent and really *do* have to be followed. But there's almost always a degree of wiggle room, and you should use your best judgment to try to make your RFP the best it can possibly be. The RFP should be simple and straightforward, and although you almost certainly will need to establish measurable benchmarks by which to judge the work, you should try to give yourself and your eventual contractor enough flexibility to work in the real world. Contracting officers sometimes don't understand that procuring a study of cultural resources is different from buying a bulldozer.

Requests for Quotes

The Buying a Bulldozer syndrome can be so severe that your agency may want you to develop not an RFP but an RFQ—a request for quotes. Obviously, it makes sense for the agency to shop around and get competitive price quotes when it needs a new bulldozer, and it can specify precisely what kind of bulldozer it wants: a 2 zillion horsepower D-94 with a Type 78 blade and an enclosed, air-conditioned cab, painted forest green with the agency logo on it. Contracting officers may assume that you can write similar specifications for your study, and then just select the outfit that says it will do it most cheaply. Needless to say, writing bulldozer procurement-type specifications for a cultural resource study is an exercise in self-deception. We do not seek a specific product—other than, perhaps, a report that meets certain more or less relevant criteria while discussing very ambiguous phenomena. We can't be sure of outcomes, and much is dependent on variables that we don't control, like the actions of consulting parties who are in no way obligated to meet our deadlines and standards. RFQs are utterly unrealistic, unless they are only for the most basic initial activities: "Give us a quote for conducting background research and holding a public meeting, on the basis of which we'll design our scoping strategy."

Set-Asides

Can you direct a contract to a particular firm? Well, it should go without saying that you shouldn't draft an RFP that only your best friend can respond to. But under United States law, there *are* legally approved ways to tip the scales in favor of particular kinds of contractors (not your best friend), and, in fact, such scale-tipping may be *mandatory*. Veteran-owned companies, for example, and especially companies owned by veterans disabled in the course of their service, have a leg up. So do companies owned by members of minority groups and by women, as well as "small" businesses—"small" being defined mostly based on volume of work. Typically, some percentage of an agency's contracts will be "set aside" for such firms, and it's often the case that *all* of an agency's cultural resource and/or environmental contracts will fall into "set-aside" categories.

You may think that one or more of these set-asides is a good idea, and perhaps that others just guarantee overly expensive, low-quality work and sweetheart deals. Having operated a small, veteran-owned, limited liability company (LLC), and having reviewed a lot of shockingly bad products of set-aside contracts, I sympathize and have mixed feelings about the whole business. But we're not likely to fix things in the foreseeable future, so be prepared to live with set-asides as best you can.

If you really think that your best friend's firm is the only one that's able to do what you need done, there may be legal ways to arrange things, but they're much too complicated to discuss here. Talk with your agency's contracting gurus.

Reviewing Proposals

So you get your RFP together and put it out to people for their responses. If you possibly can, try to avoid getting trapped into taking the low bid. There's often a very good—or from your perspective and that of the public, a very *bad*—reason why a bid is low.

Then review the proposals that come in. Be very suspicious of anyone who assures you that, yes sir or ma'am, he's going to give you just precisely what you need, no ifs, ands, or buts about it. Look for proposals that seem to reflect an understanding of what you're looking for, an understanding of the legal and administrative contexts within which you're operating, and an understanding of the physical and social environment in which the work needs to be accomplished.

Public Participation

"Social environment?" Yes. The ways that people and groups, inside and outside your agency, relate to your proposed study is critical. How things work within your agency is way beyond my ability to predict; you'll have to figure it out. Just don't assume that it's easy. Outside the agency, the key question at the outset is, will people participate, or will they not?

Yes, you *do* need outside people to participate. If you don't have their participation, you're missing a huge body of relevant information, and—very important from the standpoint of your agency—you're not enlisting affected members of the public in your enterprise, not building the relationships that will help you and your client when the time comes to consider projects and decisions that may affect them.

You can't—well, shouldn't—just send your archaeologists (or historians or architectural historians or whatever) out there to do their studies and ignore the people living in and around the area you're studying. Or they may *not* be living there, but connected to it by history, tradition, occasional use, or assumed ancestral connections. You need to try to get them to participate.

Reluctance to Participate

Why would anyone *not* want to participate in your study? Well, here are a few reasons:

1. You're not proposing to pay me anything for my generations of hard-earned knowledge.
2. I don't trust the government.
3. Some of what I know is secret. Why should I share it with you?
4. It requires investment of my time and trouble. Why should I invest?

These rationales can be very easily drawn upon to justify not cooperating, and you can't really force people to change their minds.

As a result, there's a good chance that—despite your best efforts—whatever study you'll be able to do *will* be pretty much an in-house affair. Typically, you and/or a contractor will be examining the historical and ethnographic record and doing a field survey to see what can be learned. There's nothing wrong with this, but you should try to avoid putting too much reliance on it. If you don't have buy-in from the people who value the area's cultural resources, and who are likely to get aggravated when things are done to them, your study isn't going to be worth much.

Section 110 and Section 106

I've often seen it happen that an agency will do a Section 110 survey, get little cooperation from local people, and then years later get into a Section 106 case in which they denigrate the concerns of the locals because they—the locals—didn't bring them up during the Section 110 survey. This seems to me to be a gross violation of the public trust, and simpleminded to boot. The locals had no reason to cooperate with the Section 110 survey, and they had at least the reasons listed above *not* to do so. Now there's some kind of potentially destructive project proposed—that's why you're doing a Section 106 review—and the locals have every reason to insist that you pay attention to their concerns. Totally different ball games.

A "negative" Section 110 study should *never* be relied on in a Section 106 review, except as an imperfect, incomplete body of relevant data. The same goes for a "positive" study that tells you a lot about some classes of things—say, major institutional buildings, or prehistoric village sites—but not about others. Major institutional buildings and prehistoric village sites are doubtless important, but they may not be the *only* important things subject to effect by a project. The bottom line is that Section 110 studies, and their equivalents under other legal authorities, can be useful and enlightening, but you should never take them to be authoritative.

Work done under Section 110 is not exempt from Section 106 review. So if you want to spend money under the authority of Section 110 on something that has the potential to *affect* historic places—like excavating an archaeological site, or stabilizing one that's washing down the river—you'll need to consult interested parties and seek agreement per the Section 106 regulations. This is one of those things it's smart to do in advance of having the funds to pursue the work, so that you're ready to go if and when the money becomes available (e.g., at year's end; see below). But if you do consultation in advance, and, for example, come up with an MOA that provides for excavating or stabilizing the site, you should be prepared to revisit it when it looks like the money may become available. Things do change, including how agreeable people may be about a given project or approach.

Year-End Money

Each agency of government—at least in the United States, and I suspect it's similar elsewhere—develops an annual budget, within which it works over the course of a "fiscal year," which may or may not coincide with the calendar year. It's not uncommon for an agency to come to the end of the year with a bit more money in its budget than it's readily able to spend. This is perfectly understandable; no one can predict with perfect accuracy what they'll need to spend in the course of a year.

But agencies really, really don't like to admit that they overbudgeted—though admitting it, you might think, would be a responsible thing to do—so they often wind up, as the end of the fiscal year approaches, needing to dump some money into worthwhile endeavors. Because if they don't, the fiscal watchdogs in the Office of Management and Budget (OMB) will say, "Well, hell, these guys don't need as much money as we've been giving them, so let's give them less next year." That may be perfectly true, though I, for one, would never rely on OMB analysts to make wise decisions in the matter. But regardless, your agency doesn't want its budget reduced, so near the end of the fiscal year there's likely to be a scramble to allocate year-end money. If you have a project that's ready to go—a Section 110 study, or maybe stabilizing an eroding archaeological site, or rehabilitating a historic building—you can be a hero in your agency at the end of the fiscal year, and get good work done too.

So it will serve you to set up, if you can, a sort of stockpile of ready-to-go projects—scopes of work developed, consultations performed, any necessary reviews completed under Section 106, NEPA, or other laws—that you can pull off the shelf and get underway. Of course, any such stockpile has a limited shelf life; things change, and this has to be accounted for when you pull down an old scope and dust it off. Still, having a stockpile of scopes can be a real advantage.

Keep Track

Once a contract has been let—probably to a consulting firm—to carry out the terms of the RFP you've drafted, you will need to keep track of how it's carried out. You probably won't be the contracting officer overseeing the work, but you can and should be designated the contracting officer's technical representative (COTR). Even if you're not the COTR, it should be possible for you to get wrapped into the administration of the contract so you can be aware of how the work's being done. Be alert for glitches (which aren't necessarily anyone's fault), for inefficiencies, for contractors going off on tangents. If it turns out that there's something wrong with the contract terms, or that something needs to be done that's more or less or different from what was expected, be prepared to negotiate a change order or other legally permissible adjustment to the contract. You'll need to work with your contracting officer on any change in the contract terms, to make sure that it *is* permissible.

You'll also need to ensure that reports and other products—often called "deliverables"—are delivered on time, that they're reviewed promptly, and that any necessary corrections are made. And of course—I say this as someone who's worked fairly often as a contractor for government agencies and others—make sure, if you can, that your contractors are paid in a timely way. They have payrolls and expenses to cover.

Responding to an RFP

Most people who work in CRM don't write RFPs; we *respond* to them. If you're working in a private firm in the United States, there will be somebody on staff who keeps track of the websites and other places where RFPs are published. If you're in an academic institution or museum, there will probably be a foundation office that tries to do the same thing. It's necessary to be alert, because the time made available to respond to an RFP may be quite limited—maybe 60 days or even less.

You have to respond in a form that's acceptable to whoever publishes the RFP, which means knowing the relevant acquisition regulations if it's a government agency. Responding to a request from a non-governmental body, like a mining or pipeline company, is usually easier and less bureaucratic. But regardless of who requests the work, you have to show them that you understand what they need and that you can provide it. Often this will require you—or somebody—to recruit other firms, institutions, or organizations as partners, which of course introduces additional layers of complexity.

If none of this seems like a lot of fun, I sympathize. It's part of the price of doing stuff like CRM in a system dominated by big, complex institutions and organized around capitalist principles. There are probably better ways to get the job done, but for now at least, this is what we have to work with in the United States

For the record, I almost never respond to RFPs any more, and very seldom work for government agencies or project proponents. But that's because I'm an old guy with a modest retirement income and can afford, more or less, to work for indigenous groups, citizens groups, and non-governmental organizations. I find this a lot easier (if less remunerative).

Construction (and Other) Monitoring

"Construction monitoring" means having presumably trained and competent people on-site during construction of a highway, pipeline, mine, or other project, who can step in and preserve anything that's discovered. In the United States, there are often "archaeological monitors" and "Native American monitors"—the former to be alert to artifacts and other things an archaeologist can recognize, the latter to represent the interests of one or more local tribes.

Construction monitoring can be a useful part of a mitigation program. *After you've done everything else that's reasonable to do* (identification/evaluation, impact avoidance/reduction through project design, data recovery, etc.), and the bulldozers begin to roll, it may be a good idea to have someone knowledgeable on hand to see what's turned up, and to recover things and data where possible. A monitor is also helpful when the situation is stubbornly ambiguous—you've done everything reasonable to figure out what's there, you haven't found anything, but you're still not comfortable saying there's *nothing* there.

If you're going to provide for monitoring, make sure that its carefully described in whatever MOA or work plan is agreed upon. What will the monitors' qualifications be? Their work hours, their training in safety procedures? What equipment will they have, and, particularly, what will be their rights and responsibilities? Can they close down construction? Stop the digging? For how long? While doing what? What happens when their time runs out? Can anything be done by construction workers when monitors *aren't* around? If so, what? What happens to anything the monitors collect? And, of course, who pays them? All these things need to be thought out, usually negotiated, and put in writing so everyone understands the ground rules. *In advance!*

Sometimes monitors are employed outside the context of construction. For example, in California, Native American monitors are sometimes hired to accompany archaeological and other specialist field crews, presumably to be alert for things the non-Native specialists may not know enough to spot, and/ or just to keep the specialists honest.

The big problem with monitoring, I think—at least in California where it's endemic under the California Environmental Quality Act (CEQA)—is that it's sometimes adopted as a *substitute* for all that tedious identification and

evaluation and effect determination and consultation stuff. So your development may take out an ancient living site, or go through an area where such a
site is suspected? No problem, we'll provide for monitoring, and all will be well!

Of course, this is nonsense. It's like saying, "We don't need to look before
we jump off this ledge, because if it turns out to be 400 meters to the bottom,
we'll have people down there to scrape us off the pavement." The idea of the
environmental *assessment* required by the NEPA (and the CEQA) and the
"taking into account" required by Section 106 of the NHPA—and by similar
legal authorities worldwide—is to *assess* impacts, to consider them *before* you
decide whether and how to let them happen.

Substituting monitoring for all that planning and consultation vitiates the
whole purpose of the NEPA, NHPA, CEQA, and their kin. But it's popular
with developers; it lets them, in effect, buy their way out of actually "taking
into account" and mitigating the impacts of their projects. And some archaeologists, Indian tribes, and other communities have bought into it—perhaps
because they don't know better, perhaps because it's easy money. I think it's
pretty sad.

Composing Nominations

In chapter 3 and earlier in this chapter, I was pretty dismissive of preparing
nominations to lists like the National Register of Historic Places (NRHP), but
some CRM archaeologists—and many more historians, architectural historians, and other specialists—spend a lot of time doing exactly that. It's necessary
in some countries and under the laws of some cities, states, and other jurisdictions in this country, where nothing gets "taken into account" in planning
unless and until someone's successfully nominated it. But it's a terrible pain
in the backside, usually about as interesting as composing a user's manual for
your trowel, and under United States federal law—if that law's being carried
out sensibly—it's almost always a waste of time (see chapter 3). You may be
called upon to do it, though, and if you point out that it's a waste of time and
money, you'll often be looked at as if you're speaking Klingon.

If you're required to nominate something, bone up on the rules and regulations and guidelines that pertain to doing so. In the United States, these are
published by the National Park Service (NPS) and the various State Historic
Preservation Officers (SHPOs). Follow them to the letter, and be very cautious
about exhibiting any creativity; it's usually neither understood nor appreciated.

Keeping Secrets

CRM is a public activity; it's done on behalf of the public, in the public interest. But in carrying it out, we're often expected—rightly or wrongly—to keep

secrets. It's important to think about when, how, and especially whether secrecy is really necessary and desirable—even if it's being jammed down our throats.

Confidentiality

Several United States laws, and presumably similar laws in other countries, require that information on archaeological sites, historic buildings, and sometimes other "cultural resources" be kept confidential, based on the not unjustified fear that if you let the public know where these sensitive places are, people will dig them up or knock them down or smear graffiti on them or go watch the rituals that may be carried out there. Sometimes, indeed, that fear *is* justified, but too often it's allowed to rationalize keeping information secret that doesn't remotely need to be kept secret—unless you define "need" in a very self-serving way: by keeping secrets we can keep people from knowing that we're destroying things that are culturally important. I've had this happen to me. I hear that the Agency for Hardrock Management (AHM) is about to allow BigDig Minerals to excavate a rhyolite ridge that may be sacred to the RidgeWatcher Tribe. I inquire about it. "Sorry," says AHM, "we can't talk about it. Too sacred." But not too sacred to be mined.

Yes, that's extreme, and there are ways to fight or get around it. But it's the kind of thing I've seen happen, and as a CRM archaeologist you may be expected to collaborate in it. You may have to come to grips with whether to do so, and with what alternatives you can find.

Non-Disclosure Agreements (NDAs)

If you're working for a private firm, and sometimes even in the public sector, you may be expected to sign non-disclosure agreements (NDAs)—that is, agreements not to tell anybody about the work you're doing, or what you're learning. I detest and abhor NDAs as a matter of principle, but I have to acknowledge that sometimes they're necessary, for example:

- When you're employed as an expert witness in a court case. Even though your testimony is supposed to be objective and "true" to the best of your knowledge and belief, your client is going to deploy it in accordance with her or his litigation strategy, and understandably doesn't want you spilling the beans in advance, especially to the opposition.
- When you're employed on a project whose results are likely to be announced at a press conference or revealed in the media. Your client naturally wants your information to remain quiet until the time is ripe to spring it on the breathlessly waiting world.
- When you're working with really special technology or methods to which your client has proprietary rights.
- When your work bears significantly on matters of national defense.

- When revealing the results of your work would seriously risk harm to people, animals, other aspects of the environment, or cultural resources.

In cases like these, it may be appropriate for your client to insist that you sign an agreement saying that for some period of time you won't disclose what you're doing, or what results you've achieved.

But some companies—and, probably, government agencies—allow or cause these reasonable non-disclosure situations to balloon into requirements that one never disclose anything about anything, ever. An NDA I'm reviewing right now prohibits those who sign it from *ever* revealing anything about the following:

- the project(s) on which they're working;
- the identity of their client(s);
- their client's project(s);
- their work's regulatory context(s);
- how their work is conducted;
- whom they consulted (if anyone); and
- the results of their work.

All in perpetuity, with no wiggle room. It also sneaks in a "non-compete" clause, prohibiting the employee who signs it from working for anyone who competes with the firm that promulgates the NDA. And "competition" is rather softly defined. So is, say, an environmental group that's critical of the firm's work a competitor? It's up to the courts, I suppose.

It should go without saying that this sort of thing is utterly inconsistent with any kind of professional practice that even pretends to be done in the public interest, as CRM routinely does. It seems to me a pretty strange way to do science, too, though I guess 'secret science" isn't a complete oxymoron. But lots of companies and organizations seem to promulgate highly restrictive NDAs without a second thought, and their prospective employees, desperate for paychecks, feel they have little choice but to agree.

I strongly encourage you *not* to agree too readily. Don't assume that "your secrecy or your life" NDAs are the natural way of the business world. Sadly, they're increasingly common, but there's nothing *necessary* about them. And depending on how they're worded, they may even be illegal; non-competition provisions have had particularly checkered histories in some state courts. Don't automatically buy the assurance that NDAs are just part of the way everybody does business. They're not—yet, anyway. Ask questions; challenge what's thrust in your face. My usual practice is to ask why each secrecy provision is necessary, and how long or under what conditions it's necessary. Usually, when everyone thinks about it, everyone can agree that secrecy needn't be maintained for more than a year, or for the duration of the litigation, or that an exception can be made for replies to public information requests, or whatever makes sense under the circumstances. Then you write that condition into the NDA, and everyone can sign it in good conscience.

Study Questions

1. When might construction monitoring be a good idea? A bad idea?
2. Suppose you're working for a United States government agency and you want to renovate an old military barracks building to serve as an archaeology lab. What standards and guidelines should you consider, and how might doing so influence your renovation work?
3. Suppose you're working for a United States government land management agency, which finds itself with $200,000 that it needs to commit to something worthwhile before the end of the fiscal year. What will you need to do if you want to snag this money for an important archaeological project?
4. Go to http://cbd-net.com/index.php/search/ and search for "archaeological" (or another term of your choice). See what RFPs pop up. Select one and discuss how you might respond to it.
5. When and why would you invest your own money in getting something listed on an official register of cultural resources like the NRHP? What alternatives would you explore, if any?
6. Would you sign a non-disclosure agreement? Why or why not?

Note

1. The "committee," which was never formally constituted, advised Senator Wyche Fowler (D-GA), the amendment's major sponsor. It included representatives of the NPS, ACHP, National Trust for Historic Preservation, and National Conference of SHPOs, which kindly gave me a seat at the table.

Further Reading

FAR (Federal Acquisition Regulations). n.d. https://www.acquisition.gov/browsefar.
As the name implies, the regulations governing United States government acquisition of everything from mousepads to moon rockets.

FedBizOps (formerly Commerce Business Daily). n.d. http://cbd-net.com/.
The website where requests for proposals (RFPs) are listed by United States federal agencies and some others. Scheduled to be replaced in 2020 by beta. SAM.gov.

Hester, Randolph T. 2010. *Design for Ecological Democracy.* Cambridge, MA: MIT Press.
Hester's work on the "sacred structure" of communities like Manteo, North Carolina, has broken important ground in participatory and culturally sensitive land-use planning.

Nabatchi, Tina, and Matt Leighninger. 2015. *Public Participation for 21st Century Democracy.* San Francisco: Jossey-Bass.
General treatment of the roles and challenges of public participation in government operations like land and resource management.

United States Secretary of the Interior. n.d. *Standards and Guidelines for Federal Agency Preservation Programs Pursuant to the National Historic Preservation Act.* https://www.energy.gov/nepa/downloads/secretary-interiors-standards-and-guidelines-federal-agency-historic-preservation.

>   These "Standards and Guidelines" are oriented largely toward compliance with Section 110 of the United States National Historic Preservation Act.

United States Small Business Administration. 2015. *Government Contracting 101.* https://www.sba.gov/sites/default/files/gc101-1_workbook.pdf.

>   An introduction to United States government contracting.

Chapter 7

Special Cases and Loose Ends

CRM is a thing of rags and tatters, a hodge-podge of ideas, assumptions, procedures, and practices drawn from multiple scholarly and non-scholarly disciplines and cobbled together by legislative, regulatory, and semi-academic entities, often with little knowledge of or interest in its intellectual underpinnings. Generally speaking, CRM organizes itself into the topics addressed in chapters 2 through 6: consultation, identification, evaluation, assessing effects, resolving adverse effects, and general management. But even after cramming miscellaneous stuff like nominations to lists, monitoring, and signing (or not signing) NDAs into the "general management" category, there are special cases to address and loose ends to tie up. Important among these are how we deal with disasters, the particulars of working in places like house museums and parks, being an activist and going to court, and doing CRM as a business.

Disasters

Natural (or unnatural) disasters like fires, floods, and acts of war present special problems for CRM. Some disasters just can't be very effectively dealt with; as far as I know, there was no realistic way for the site managers at Palmyra in Syria to prevent the Daesh[1] from blowing the place up. There are UN agreements that theoretically commit warring nations to protect aspects of physical cultural heritage, but particularly in recent years, as non-state actors have become seriously involved in war making, the effectiveness of these institutions has become shaky at best. Earthquakes, volcanic eruptions, and meteor/comet strikes are other examples of disasters about which little can be done to conserve cultural resources—though a good deal can be done to *prepare* for things like earthquakes, so "seismic retrofit" has become a growth industry among historical architects and engineers.

Fires

In the United States, most land-managing agencies have developed pretty sophisticated ways to address the cultural effects of things like wildfires. Archaeologists and sometimes Indian tribal specialists are assigned to be members of fire crews.

If you become a "fire archaeologist"—as is usual in CRM—you'll need to know about and do things besides archaeology. For one thing, obviously, you'll be working on and with firefighting teams, so you need to learn firefighting methods and teamwork, and stay in top physical condition. For another, you'll have to be concerned with cultural resources that—while tangible—aren't exactly archaeological. Buildings and other structures are usually more or less flammable. You'll be removing trees and brush ("fuel") around them and wrapping them in flame-retardant fabric. The same applies with carved trees (dendroglyphs);[2] trees that show evidence of use to make bows, arrows, and the like; and trees that are simply identified as culturally important. Finding such flammable cultural resources, and locating them accurately so you can get to them quickly in case of fire, is a really good reason for doing targeted field surveys and consultations. Rock art is also susceptible to fire damage; you may need to remove fuel close to rock art sites and find ways to screen them before the flames arrive. Likewise with ruins that protrude from the ground.

Subsurface archaeological sites may not be too vulnerable to fire, though surface artifacts will certainly be damaged. Archaeological sites are very vulnerable to damage by firefighting itself, so fire archaeologists often work with firefighting teams to route the bulldozers and other heavy equipment away from sensitive sites. Knowing where those sites are is another excellent reason to do surveys and consultations.

FEMA

In the United States, the Federal Emergency Management Agency (FEMA) has a network of CRM experts to assist with situations where historic places are at risk. I know people who've worked with FEMA, and my impression is that it's satisfying work. You get to try to help people save places that are important to them from floods, hurricanes, wildfires, the effects of earthquakes, and the like, and/or to recover from such disasters. FEMA is also involved in helping communities *prepare* for emergencies—notably, these days, emergencies related to the climate crisis. This can present some serious challenges. Many towns and cities were built on floodplains or the coast, for obvious reasons, and their locations now make them vulnerable. How can we make them—and the wetlands and rural areas surrounding them—safe from impending disaster without sacrificing what their people regard as important to their history, their heritage, their identity? *Can* we do so? Or can we manage the retreat of communities from endangered places, in ways that respect their cultural values and ways of life? My impression is that FEMA is making a real effort, and that the various historic preservation authorities (SHPOs, ACHP, NPS) are cooperating, but it also strikes me that what's being done is pretty ad hoc. We're likely to be looking at some really serious losses down the road.

Meanwhile, the oceans are rising and eating away at the shorelines—to say nothing of island nations like Kiribati and Tuvalu, the Marshall Islands, parts of the Federated States of Micronesia, and the Maldives—and carrying away archaeological sites, places of cultural significance, and even historic buildings and communities. I'm not aware of any systematic effort that's underway to address these ongoing emergencies, except by those island nations that are variously looking to relocate their people (with attendant cultural losses), somehow build and maintain floating communities, or just fill sandbags and plant mangroves. In Alaska, where erosion of coastal archaeological sites is a big issue, some substantial rescue archaeology programs have been undertaken, and there are quite a few efforts being made at least to document the effects of climate change on various kinds of cultural resources (notably archaeological sites). But I don't know of any such program that's organized on a regional or agency-wide basis. And monitoring effects is one thing; doing anything about them is something else again. The NPS has put out some thoughtful ideas and case studies, but I haven't seen a whole lot being done about them.

Working in Parks, House Museums, etc.

Some CRM archaeologists work in national, regional, state, tribal, and local parks and sometimes in historic sites and house museums. Particularly in national parks in the United States, their responsibilities are not unlike those of archaeologists employed in other land-managing agencies, except that they may be more involved in public interpretation. In parks, historic sites, and house museums not managed by the National Park Service or another federal agency, their responsibilities may be pretty diverse and range right down to cleaning restrooms and washing windows. The advantage of this kind of work, I think, is that you have a lot of opportunities to interact with people, and may be able to take part in some innovative forms of public interpretation and public involvement. The disadvantages, as I understand them, include typically low pay and rather precarious job security.

Being an Activist

It doesn't pay well—or at all—but there's a real need for people to be activists for CRM, that is, for the management of cultural resources. And often for their salvation.

A vanishingly small percentage of trained CRM people work for organizations that actively promote the management of cultural resources, such as the National Trust for Historic Preservation[3] in the United States and its equivalents in the United Kingdom[4] and elsewhere; for the Archaeological Conservancy;[5] or for groups with broader missions that include concern for cultural resources, such as the Native American Rights Fund,[6] Cultural Survival,[7] Survival International,[8] and the Sustainable Preservation Initiative.[9] If you work for such an organization, you won't make much money, and you'll likely work your tail off. But it can be rewarding, challenging, and make you feel good about yourself.

Many CRM specialists also work as activists on the more or less local level, often as a sideline to their "day jobs" in academia or the professional CRM/EIA industry. This too can be rewarding (though seldom if ever remunerative), but you have to be careful not to mix up your functions and stumble over your own feet. If you're active in "Stop the Big Blue River Dam," it may not be a great idea to seek a contract from the Big Blue River Dam and Power Company. My alliances with Indian tribes in California in the 1970s made me *persona non grata* to the development interests whose contracts were and are the bread and butter of the state's then-developing CRM "industry." I don't regret those alliances, and I have serious qualms about developer-financed CRM. But there's no question that my tilt toward advocacy had impacts on my livelihood and the well-being of my family. My children say they've forgiven me; I'd like to believe them.

Going to Court

Whether as an activist or as the employee of an agency or a CRM or EIA firm, you may find that you need or want to testify in court. This does not have to be a scary experience; I find it to be kind of fun, if tedious at times. But there are rules by which you need to abide.

You're typically working closely with one or more attorneys, and you need to pay close attention to the rules of the road that they lay out. Don't talk about the case without their permission. Don't share documents without their permission. They're trying to make a case, and your job is to help them, or at least not undercut them. *As long as the case they're trying to make is one you can live with.*

If they want you to testify that the Big Blue River Dam is just peachy-keen from a CRM perspective when you know it will destroy a bunch of archaeological sites or flood the places where local people traditionally hunt muskrat—or if you just *don't know* what impact it will have—you certainly shouldn't go along with their requests. The lawyers shouldn't ask you to lie.

A lawsuit is inherently adversarial, so you'll usually be called by one side or the other. That doesn't mean that you have to say what that side's lawyers want you to say, but you don't want to surprise them. If you've given the lawyers who called you reason to think that nobody hunts muskrats along the Big Blue, you ought not then tell the court that they do—unless you've just learned that they do, and have given the lawyers who called you as much advance warning as you can.

You may or may not actually wind up on the witness stand. I've been in a dozen or so court cases—maybe more—and have been on the stand only a handful of times. Most times you'll prepare written depositions or declarations, and sometimes you'll be "deposed"—I know, a funny word—by attorneys for both sides with a court reporter recording everything—or maybe video-recording it all. This is more or less like being on the stand in that each set of attorneys gets to ask you things and object to one another's questions. It can be kind of a kick, especially if you're being paid to sit there and listen to the lawyers bicker before answering their questions.

You need to be careful to answer only the question that's asked. Don't elaborate unless you're asked to. If you're asked whether, according to your research, people hunt muskrat along the Big Blue River, say, "Yes, based on my research it appears that they do," or "No, based on my research it appears that they don't." Don't extemporize—about how sad it is that muskrats have been wiped out in the Big Blue watershed, or how great it is because you hate muskrats—unless you're asked to do so. If it's important, the lawyers will ask you. If they're doing their jobs.

And of course, the bottom line is that you have to tell the truth, the whole truth, and nothing but the truth. And if you don't think you know what the truth is—which in a field as soft and squishy as CRM is often the case—it's perfectly proper to say so.

The Business End of It All

A lot of academic CRM programs whose curricula I've seen emphasize what amounts to "doing archaeology as a business": bringing in people from local CRM firms to talk about responding to RFPs, adhering to government regulations, and handling personnel issues. This seems to me to miss the major point of CRM, which (I know I'm beating a dead horse) is *not* just doing archaeology in a business environment. But there's no question that doing CRM—at least for those of us outside government—does involve being businesslike, and often working in and even running businesses. This means having to be alert to things you may not have had to consider in an academic milieu, such as the following:

1. You or your employer will be responding to RFPs. You need to know the rules for doing so, or have someone in your organization who does.
2. You or your employer will probably be hiring and firing people, which involves you in a host of administrative activities, many with cost implications. You have to deal with unemployment insurance, payroll, tax withholding, and tax reporting.
3. Having employees inevitably involves you in employee relations. You or your employer need to know about and respect fair employment practices, avoid even the appearance of bias based on race, gender, or sexual orientation, and

be alert to the possibility of harassment on any such grounds—heading it off if possible, addressing it if it's alleged.

4. At the same time, you or your employer will have the responsibility and opportunity to participate in and develop affirmative action programs, giving opportunities to minorities and people with special needs and abilities. In the United States and some other countries, CRM tends to be a dreadfully white-skinned affair, and that needs to change. At the same time, there are people with special needs who can play important roles in your organization if you give them the chance. For example, disabled veterans working through programs such as the Veterans Curation Program,[10] Veterans HistoriCorps,[11] or Veterans Conservation Corps[12] in the United States and Breaking Ground Heritage[13] in the United Kingdom have skills that your firm may very well be able to put to work.[14] One of my life's regrets is that I was never able to follow up on a small pilot project we did in California during my grad school days, involving hearing-impaired students in archaeological fieldwork. They were superb.

5. You'll be in competition with other firms, many of which may be run by friends and colleagues—or by the guy who could never maintain straight sidewalls in field school. You'll need to figure out how to compete in a collegial manner, both with those you respect and with those you think ought to be—well, doing something else. And because few firms can maintain staff to handle every possible kind of CRM issue, you may often find it necessary to form multi-firm teams to respond to an RFP—and to carry out the work if that response is successful.

All this requires knowledge of business practices, business ethics, business law, and/or people in or around your organization who can advise you. By being totally without ambition to succeed in the CRM business, I've been able to get by with a good outside payroll/tax service and a very part-time business manager.[15] But if you aspire to bigger things, you'll have to think bigger than I have.

Study Questions

1. Suppose you're working for a United States government agency that manages land on the seacoast, and you notice that due to erosion caused by sea level rise, archaeological sites are falling into the ocean. What steps can you take to address this situation? What laws, regulations, standards, and guidelines may be relevant? What governmental and other programs? What obstacles and pitfalls will you need to consider?

2. Go to https://cdxnodengn.epa.gov/cdx-enepa-public/action/eis/search and scroll down to "EISs open for comment." Click on the link and scroll down; select an environmental impact statement (EIS) that looks interesting. Imagine yourself as an activist who wants to oppose the project because of its impacts on cultural resources. What do you need to learn about the project and its effects in order to be an effective advocate?

3. Review the court decision at http://earthjustice.org/sites/default/files/files/order-denying-PI.pdf. Do you think the decision was correct? If you were asked to help challenge it in a higher court, what do you think you might do?

4. Imagine yourself as the head of a private CRM firm in the United States, staffed almost entirely by archaeologists. The Department of Veterans Affairs (https://en.wikipedia.org/wiki/United_States_Department_of_Veterans_Affairs) has posted an RFP seeking a firm to assist it with all its CRM responsibilities throughout the country. Proposals have to be in the Department's hands within 60 days. If you want to compete for this work, what do you think you will need to do?

Notes

1. Known to some as the Islamic State or ISIS, but like many others I won't so dignify them.

2. Dendroglyphs are especially well-known in New Zealand (see https://en.wikipedia.org/wiki/Arborglyph), but they're found elsewhere as well.

3. https://savingplaces.org/.

4. https://www.nationaltrust.org.uk/.

5. https://www.archaeologicalconservancy.org/.

6. https://www.narf.org/.

7. https://www.culturalsurvival.org/.

8. https://www.survivalinternational.org/.

9. http://www.sustainablepreservation.org/, which receives this book's royalties.

10. https://www.mvs.usace.army.mil/Missions/Veterans-Curation-Program/.

11. https://www.thesca.org/serve/program/veterans-historicorps.

12. https://www.dva.wa.gov/program/veterans-conservation-corp.

13. http://www.breakinggroundheritage.org.uk/.

14. Oddly (I guess), I find no similar programs in Australia, China, India, or Russia, but I may not be using the right search terms.

15. My son Thomas S. King, to whom I proffer my gratitude in lieu of decent compensation.

Further Reading

Disasters

Aguilar, Antonio. 2016. "The Seismic Rehabilitation of Historic Buildings." https://www.nps.gov/tps/how-to-preserve/briefs/41-seismic-rehabilitation.htm.
United States National Park Service guidance on seismic retrofit of historic buildings to protect against earthquake damage.

FEMA (Federal Emergency Management Agency). 2005. Integrating Historic Property and Cultural Resource Considerations into Hazard Mitigation Planning. State and Local Mitigation Planning How-To Guide. FEMA 386-6. https://www.fema.gov/pdf/fima/386-6_Book.pdf.

Guidelines for community planning to address management of the impacts of disasters on physical cultural resources.

FEMA n.d. "Natural and Cultural Resources Recovery Support Function." https://www.fema.gov/pdf/recoveryframework/natural_cultural_resources_rsf.pdf.
Description of FEMA's program to help communities prepare for and recover from the effects of disasters on their natural and cultural resources.

Florida Public Archaeology Network. n.d. "Heritage Monitoring Scouts." https://fpan.us/projects/HMSflorida.php.
A cooperative, inter-institutional citizen science-focused program that tries to monitor and address the impacts of sea level rise on archaeological sites in Florida.

Gassaway, Linn. n.d. *Fire Archaeology.* http://firearchaeology.com/Home.html.
A very useful website with lots of information about taking care of archaeological sites and historic structures in advance of and during wildfires. Many helpful links as well.

Look, David, Terry Wong, and Sylvia Rose Augustus. n.d. "The Seismic Retrofit of Historic Buildings." Old House Web. http://www.oldhouseweb.com/how-to-advice/the-seismic-retrofit-of-historic-buildings.shtml.
Advice about how to rehabilitate historic buildings and structures to minimize vulnerability to earthquake damage.

National Park Service. 2016. "Cultural Resources Climate Change Strategy." https://www.nps.gov/subjects/climatechange/culturalresourcesstrategy.htm.
Seems like a good-faith effort at addressing climate change issues. What's being done with it is anyone's guess.

Society for California Archaeology. n.d. "Climate Change and California Archaeology Studies." https://scahome.org/sca-climate-change-and-california-archaeology-studies/.
A cooperative, inter-institutional citizen science-focused program that tries to monitor and address the impacts of sea level rise on archaeological sites in California.

UNESCO. n.d. "Armed Conflict and Heritage." http://www.unesco.org/new/en/culture/themes/armed-conflict-and-heritage/.
International agreements about controlling the impacts of war on physical cultural resources; standards and guidelines, links.

United States Government Accountability Office. 2007. "Climate Change: Agencies Should Develop Guidance for Addressing the Effects on Federal Land and Water Resources." GAO-07-863. Washington, DC. https://www.gao.gov/products/GAO-07-863.
Report of an interagency workshop, with recommendations.

Williams, A. R. 2017. "Alaska's Thaw Reveals—and Threatens—a Culture's Artifacts." *National Geographic*, April. https://www.nationalgeographic.com/magazine/2017/04/artifact-melt-alaska-archaeology-climate-change/.

> Exemplary account of what climate change is doing to archaeological sites and traditional places, and what some are trying to do in response.

Being an Activist/Going to Court

Baier, Lowell E. 2015. *Inside the Equal Access to Justice Act: Environmental Litigation and the Crippling Battle over America's Lands, Endangered Species, and Critical Habitats*. New York: Rowman & Littlefield.

> Mostly about things other than cultural resources (except as very broadly construed), but has useful perspectives on environmental litigation generally.

King, Thomas F. (2007) 2016. *Saving Places That Matter: A Citizen's Guide to the National Historic Preservation Act*. New York: Routledge.

> As the title indicates, my effort to provide a guide to the NHPA for use by activists.

King, Thomas F. (2009) 2016. *Our Unprotected Heritage: Whitewashing the Destruction of Our Cultural and Natural Environment*. New York: Routledge.

> My ill-tempered diatribe about the prostitution of our environmental and cultural resource laws.

The Business End

American Cultural Resources Association. n.d. "About ACRA." http://www.acra-crm.org/.

> ACRA is an organization of CRM firms, mostly in the United States doing archaeological and historic preservation work for clients under the NEPA and NHPA. ACRA is very much about the business end of CRM, including professional standards and business practices. See especially its webinars at http://www.acra-crm.org/webinarsondemand.

Breaking Ground Heritage Corp. n.d. "Breaking Ground Heritage: Background." http://breakinggroundheritage.org.uk/.

> This community interest company, organized by military veterans in the United Kingdom (UK), uses archaeology and other aspects of heritage to help veterans make the transition to civilian employment and recover from the ill effects of their service.

Stapp, Darby C., and Julia G. Longenecker. (2009) 2016. *Avoiding Archaeological Disasters: A Risk Management Approach*. New York: Routledge.

> Explains why considering cultural resources in planning is good business.

Student Conservation Association. n.d. "Veterans HistoriCorps." https://www.thesca.
org/serve/program/veterans-historicorps.
> The website of the Veterans HistoriCorps, a national program in the United
> States aimed at using historic preservation—particularly work on historic
> buildings and structures—to help veterans acclimate to the civilian world and
> gain skills that can help them obtain and hold jobs.

United States Army Corps of Engineers. n.d. "Veterans Curation Project: Heroes Preserving History." https://veteranscurationprogram.org/.
> The website of the Veterans Curation Project, which uses curatorial work on
> archaeological collections to train military veterans in a variety of useful life
> skills.

Chapter 8

Examples of Worldwide Cultural Resource/ Heritage Management

Introduction

Recognizing that my perspective on CRM, and that of my several American collaborators, is limited by the fact that we've spent most or all of our careers in this country, I asked several colleagues from other countries to review this book's manuscript in draft and comment briefly on how practice in their nations or regions varies from ours. The commentary below doesn't pretend to be a comprehensive summary of worldwide CRM practice, but I hope it gives a taste of what things are like beyond the borders of the United States.

— • —

Archaeology and CRM in Australia

Caitlin Allen

What Is CRM in Australia and Who Does It?

Archaeological practice in Australia developed within the Western, specifically European and American traditions of both archaeology and heritage conservation, with dedicated heritage legislation in place in most jurisdictions by the end of the 1970s. Although cultural resource management or CRM is not a common term used in Australia, where "cultural heritage management" or simply "heritage management" is generally used, many of the underlying principles of the heritage management systems in Australia and the United States are the same. In essence, Australia has a well-established values-based heritage management system that is administered through a series of statutory and non-statutory protections and guidelines, supported by a well-populated network of professional heritage practitioners, including archaeologists, heritage architects, historians, interpreters, planners, and general heritage specialists.

Although in reality there are blurred lines between different types of heritage places and their associated practices of management, the broad categories of Indigenous, historic, maritime, and natural heritage are used in Australia. The work of archaeologists falls primarily into the first three groups, which are considered specialist fields in their own right, although increasing numbers of practitioners are skilled in more than one area through university training and on-the-job experience.

It is difficult in some ways to disentangle the job description of Australian archaeologists from the practices of heritage managers as a whole. This is especially the case in the last 20 years or so when there has been a shift from thinking of archaeological sites (especially the resources below ground) primarily as a source of information to thinking of them as places that may have a range of heritage values that need to be managed. Private archaeological consulting firms have responded by becoming increasingly multidisciplinary, incorporating people with skills in history, interpretation, design, architectural conservation, industrial heritage, landscape heritage, and heritage planning and policy. The nature of their work has therefore shifted in many instances from a sole focus on salvage archaeology to include heritage management, although of course, salvage archaeology and site destruction are still the most common outcomes for Indigenous and historical archaeological sites.[1]

Day-to-day archaeological work, including assessments and responses to development proposals, is almost entirely done by private consulting firms. Archaeologists working for government agencies tend to set directions, approve, and manage. While the academic sector does do archaeological research, primarily in the area of Indigenous archaeology, large-scale research excavations done by institutions in other countries are rare. Academics seldom participate in the processes of everyday heritage management unless they have a dedicated consultancy group such as the Culture and Heritage Unit in the School of Social Science at the University of Queensland, which operates like a private consultancy firm on a fee-for-service basis.

The Burra Charter Process—Identify and Manage Heritage Values

Heritage management "best practice" in Australia is established by the *Australia ICOMOS Charter for Places of Cultural Significance, The Burra Charter, 2013*, commonly referred to simply as the Burra Charter. Following its release in 1979, it was very quickly adopted by all levels of government as a best practice standard and is now the key piece of heritage doctrine that underpins Australia's official heritage management system.[2] Although the Charter has been revised a number of times in response to the continuing evolution of heritage conservation philosophies and techniques, its core values-based heritage management framework and the precautionary principle of doing "as much as necessary but as little as possible" to places that have heritage significance have not changed.

The four steps in the Burra Charter process are:

1. understand the place through research and investigation;
2. assess heritage significance, using the criteria of historic, associative, social, aesthetic, and research/technical value (extended in some jurisdictions to include rarity, representativeness, integrity, and ability to demonstrate values);
3. develop management policies for the place; and
4. manage the place both in terms of ongoing conservation and maintenance and in response to proposals for change.

The significance assessment criteria established by the Charter are used not only in the context of placing heritage items on statutory and non-statutory lists.[3] It is expected that they will be used in all heritage management documents, including archaeological assessments, heritage assessments, and conservation management plans. All management decisions flow from an understanding of heritage significance. As in the United States, the principle of unbiased evaluation is important, as much as is possible in a system based on values that are mutable. It is expected that the initial phases of significance assessment and the development of basic management policies should be done without undue influence from specific proposals for change or use.

While the provisions specific to archaeology in the Burra Charter are brief, if you consider that archaeological sites are a type of heritage place, then the Charter in its entirety is applicable to the work of archaeologists. In the 1980s, Australian archaeologists Sandra Bowdler and Anne Bickford developed some additional criteria for assessing the research values of archaeological sites. They are:

1. Can this site contribute knowledge that no other site can?
2. Can this site contribute knowledge that no other resource such as documents or oral history or previous research can?
3. Is this knowledge relevant to specific or general questions about human history or behavior or some other substantive subject?[4]

In theory, these criteria have been widely used by Australian archaeologists for both historical and Indigenous sites. However, in a well-established system such as the one Australia has it can be very easy over time to do things by rote, and the effective use of these criteria to achieve substantial research and other public outcomes from archaeological labors has been called into question by numerous practitioners.[5]

Management outcomes for archaeological sites run the full spectrum from "do nothing," through various degrees of physical investigation and recording, to in situ conservation. Excavation has been the most common outcome, with in situ conservation becoming increasingly popular over the last 15 to 20 years, depending on the nature of the proposed impact and the heritage values attributed to the place. When assessing impact, the Australian heritage system considers impacts to the heritage values of the place rather than to the place itself, a subtle but important distinction. Balancing conflicting values is common and often challenging, and negotiation and facilitation forms a large part of the work of archaeologists and heritage managers in Australia, as it does elsewhere in the world.

Administration of the Heritage System—Legislation and Listings

The formal administration of heritage in Australia is arranged according to a three-tiered system of government—federal, state, and local. The bulk of this management occurs at the state and local levels.

National/Federal Government

- Management of Australia's World Heritage nomination process and oversight of management of World Heritage listed places (19 inscribed properties, with on-the-ground management occurring at the state and local levels).
- Listing of nationally significant places on the National Heritage List (113 places as of June 2018) and assessment of applications to undertake work on these places under the *Environment Protection and Biodiversity Conservation Act 1999*.
- Administration of the *Historic Shipwrecks Act 1976*, which protects shipwrecks and their associated relics that are older than 75 years and in Australian waters (state and territory agencies delegated to administer the Act on behalf of the Commonwealth).
- Listing and management of heritage items owned by the Commonwealth.

State and Territory Governments

- Listing of state-significant places (some 50,000 across Australia) and regulation of changes to these places under the relevant state-level heritage or environmental laws.
- Listing of Indigenous heritage places (estimated at about 500,000 sites across Australia, of all levels of significance) and regulation of changes to these places under the relevant state-level heritage or environmental laws.
- Administration of permit systems to control impacts to or destruction of archaeological sites (Indigenous, historic, and maritime).

- Listing and management of state-owned heritage items.
- Listing of historic shipwrecks 75 years or more in state/territory waters.
- Development of associated policy and guidelines at the state level.
- Assessment of heritage impacts associated with large-scale development projects (on both public and private land).

Local Governments

- Listing of locally significant heritage items and consideration of impacts to these through development applications under local planning regulations.

The arrangement of legislation in each state and territory varies. In some cases, all types of heritage (Indigenous, historic, maritime, and natural) are dealt with in a coordinated way in a single heritage or environmental piece of legislation. In some jurisdictions these protections are split across a number of pieces of legislation and their associated regulations. In such cases, this has had an impact on effects by creating silos of specialization in the heritage professions, particularly in regard to Indigenous and historical archaeology. Requirements to consider heritage impacts are also embodied in most state and local development planning systems. Regardless of the split and variations in details of the protections afforded, the aims of these systems are the same in each jurisdiction, since they are derived from the Burra Charter.

As in Europe, Australian heritage legislation, planning policies, and guidelines apply regardless of land tenure. This is not to say that Australia is immune from heritage laws being "switched off" in the context of certain large-scale infrastructure projects. But in general, good heritage management practice is expected of everyone.

The listing of heritage places occurs at all three levels of government administration according to the thresholds of significance that are met. Not surprisingly, the thresholds are national, state, and local level of heritage significance. In some cases a particular place may occur on all three lists. There are also lists maintained as asset registers for heritage places owned by federal and state government agencies, as well as non-statutory lists maintained by non-governmental organizations (NGOs) such as the National Trust and the Institute of Architects. For sites on statutory lists, there are legislative provisions that apply, depending on the list they sit on. These provisions include needing to apply for permission to make certain changes to a listed place and requirements to maintain them to a certain standard.

It should be noted that very few archaeological sites sit on statutory lists. The key protections for archaeological sites are contained in separate legislative provisions administered at the state level that apply to all land in that state or territory. In New South Wales (NSW), for example, a historical archaeological excavation permit is required for the disturbance or excavation of any land (under Part 6 of the *NSW Heritage Act 1977*) if it is known or reasonably suspected that the activity will or is likely to result in a relic being discovered, exposed, moved, damaged, or destroyed. A relic under the NSW Heritage Act is defined as having significance at a state or local level. In the past, the definition was based on a rolling date of 50 years and older. Some jurisdictions in Australia still have date-based definitions, but most have moved to a significance test. Permits will be issued only if there is an appropriately experienced archaeologist involved with the work, which is subject to an approved research design and excavation methodology. An Aboriginal Heritage Impact Permit under Part 6 of the *NSW National Parks and Wildlife Act 1974* is required to harm or desecrate an Aboriginal object or place anywhere in the state. As for historic heritage, the impacts must be professionally assessed and work undertaken by suitably experienced archaeologists, with an additional requirement for consultation with and involvement of relevant members of the Aboriginal community or communities. Similar requirements exist in most of the Australian states and territories. Of course, while much time and effort are invested up to the point of issuing an approval, monitoring of compliance is underfunded in most jurisdictions. There are also difficulties with public dissemination of results and finding places to house archaeological collections, many of which sit in private, inaccessible, and in some cases unknown locations. An exception to this is in the state of Victoria, which has a state-funded archaeological conservation lab that houses artifact collections from land archaeological sites, shipwrecks, and buildings with the aim of making them more accessible to the public, and for research and exhibition.

Ownership and Funding

The physical evidence associated with heritage places—buildings and/or evidence of buildings, works, objects, archaeological deposits, machinery—is usually the property of the landowner, although some jurisdictions allow for Aboriginal people to own Aboriginal human remains and certain sacred objects.[6] The Crown owns Aboriginal "movable" objects, such as stone, shell, and bone artifacts.

The cost of heritage conservation work is borne by the property owner or proponent of work to a heritage place. The government only provides funding for administering the various pieces of heritage legislation and for managing heritage places in government ownership. It also allows for a limited number of heritage grant schemes.

Communities in the Australian Heritage System

The way the official heritage management system in Australia deals with intangible, social, and spiritual heritage values is highly variable, depending on the type of heritage they are associated with. One of the key criticisms of the Burra Charter, despite assertions by Australia ICOMOS that its clauses are encompassing of all types of heritage, is that in practice it has led to a heavy emphasis on heritage fabric (the materiality of a place) at the expense of intangible values. In addition, the professionalization of heritage management over the last 40 years has served to alienate communities in many respects.[7]

Although not perfect, the acknowledgment of Indigenous cultural and spiritual values is far more sophisticated than that for non-Indigenous places. There are policies and in some cases legislative requirements for Indigenous communities to be consulted in the identification, assessment, and management of places important to them,[8] as well as guidelines that specify when and how this is to be done. Many communities are also reasserting control of their heritage, more often acting as the leaders in heritage conservation and assessment rather than people to merely be consulted.[9]

No such formal requirements exist for non-Indigenous heritage places and communities. The assessment of social values for these places is often done poorly or not at all, due to the expense and time involved in doing it well. A series of community-based heritage studies done in NSW have used communities in conjunction with experts to identify places that might be included on local heritage lists, but these are not commonplace.[10]

— • —

Cultural Resource Management in Belize

Jaime J. Awe

Similar in area to the state of Massachusetts, but with a population of only 350,000 inhabitants, Belize has a rich and diverse cultural heritage that includes both the tangible and intangible cultural remains and traditions of Pre-Ceramic people; the pre-Columbian and modern Maya; Spanish and British colonizers; African, East Indian and Asian peoples; and other more recent immigrants from around the globe. To preserve this rich heritage the government of Belize introduced heritage legislation as early as 1894. Amendments, revisions, and new regulations in the 1900s and 2000s have resulted in one of the most comprehensive heritage management systems in Central America. Today, the legal responsibility for managing cultural resources lies with the four departments or branches of Belize's National Institute of Culture and History (NICH), a quasi-government institution. These four branches include the Institute of Archaeology (IA), the Institute of Creative Arts (ICA), the Institute of Social and Cultural Research (ISCR), and the Museum of Belize (MOB) and its Houses of Cultures (HOCs).

Heritage Legislation in Belize

The management of cultural resources in Belize is best described as a unitary or centralized system of management. What this means is that, unlike the United States where there are different sets of regulations governing the ownership and management of heritage on private, state, and federal lands, Belize has a single body of legislation for the protection, conservation, and management of all cultural resources in the country. This legislation, known as the National Institute of Culture and History (NICH) Act, Chapter 331 of the Subsidiary Laws of Belize, was enacted in 2000 and revised in 2003. A major accomplishment of the NICH Act is that it brought together, under one umbrella, four previous independent government departments that were historically responsible for the preservation and promotion of Belizean culture in all its manifestations. At the head of the institution is the president of NICH, who oversees the four branches of the organization. Each branch is headed by a director who, along with staff, executes the specific responsibilities of the respective institutions.

The Four Branches of Belize's National Institute of Culture and History

As noted above, the National Institute of Culture and History comprises four branches or departments. The Institute of Creative Arts (ICA) is one of the newest and is headquartered in Belize City, the most populous community in the country. The primary responsibility of the ICA is to manage all forms of creative cultural expression, including dance, music, theater, visual arts, and writing. The ICA hosts regular live performances at the Bliss Center for the Performing Arts and works closely with the Ministry of Education and Culture to encourage training in all subdisciplines of the creative arts across the country. The ICA also curates collections of art, musical performances, and films; maintains an inventory of musical productions; and is a leading member of the Belize Book Industry Association. All commercial and documentary films recorded in Belize must acquire permits from the ICA, and must include a local agent in the production of the film.

The Institute of Social and Cultural Research (ISCR) is responsible for the management of Belize's intangible cultural heritage, and for promoting research and publications that focus on this type of heritage. The ISCR works closely with ethnic organizations across the country, including the National Kriol Council in Belize City, the East Indian Council in northern Belize, the

National Garifuna Council in south-central Belize, and Maya Councils in southern Belize. The ISCR also collaborates and maintains close ties with the Belize History Association, the National Library System, the National Archives and Record Service, and the Belize Book Industry Association. Since its inception, the ISCR has had responsibility for implementing the 2003 UNESCO Convention for the Safeguarding of the Intangible Cultural Heritage. This type of heritage includes, but is not limited to, oral traditions, social practices, local rituals and festive events, and traditional craftsmanship. Information on all these types of intangible heritage is recorded and inventoried at the ISCR headquarters in Belize's capital city of Belmopan. The ISCR also issues permits for cultural anthropological research in the country, archives anthropological reports produced by these projects, and holds an annual symposium for anthropologists and historians.

The Museum of Belize (MOB) is responsible for curating and exhibiting the country's portable tangible heritage, and for educational programs that inform the public of Belize's rich and diverse cultural heritage. The MOB also manages the Museum of Belize City, oversees Houses of Cultures (HOCs) in seven of the eight major towns in the country, and works in close collaboration with the Institute of Archaeology and the city councils of the six districts (states) of Belize. The Houses of Cultures generally operate as small community-based museums where portable objects associated with local ethnic groups can be exhibited, and where local traditions can be re-enacted and displayed. Today, a major goal of the MOB is to design a national museum for Belize that will be based in Belmopan.

The Institute of Archaeology (IA) is the oldest branch of NICH. Previously known as the Department of Archaeology, this institution is charged with the protection, preservation, and management of Belize's ancient monuments and antiquities. Under the NICH Act, all "ancient monuments" and "antiquities" are the property of the nation's government, regardless of whether those monuments and antiquities are situated on private or public property. The NICH Act defines ancient monuments as "any structure or building erected by man or any natural feature transformed or worked by man, or the remains or any part thereof, whether upon any land or in any river, stream or watercourse or under the territorial waters of Belize, that has been in existence for one hundred years or more." Antiquities are defined as "any article manufactured or worked by man, whether of stone, pottery, metal, wood, glass, or any other substance, or any part thereof" that was produced by the ancient Maya, or any other civilization, "being of an age of one hundred years or more."

One of the key mandates of the Institute of Archaeology, also enshrined in the NICH Act, is the imposition of conditions on all types of archaeological work or investigations. In order to acquire a research permit, for example, prospective principal investigators must meet several key requirements. These include, but are not limited to, (1) having a PhD, (2) being affiliated with an accredited institution (e.g., a university or museum), (3) providing proof of adequate funding to

conduct the research described in the proposal, (4) having permission of landowners if the project is to be conducted on private property, and (5) providing
the names and curricula vitae of foreign personnel. In addition, first-time appli-
cants must provide three letters of reference from established archaeologists.
Research permits are generally valid for a calendar year, and subsequent renew-
als are issued only if permit holders have submitted annual progress reports
and proof of adequate funding to continue their projects. Since 2000, there
have been approximately 20 research permits issued each year. The principal
investigators of these projects continue to be predominantly from United States
institutions, with a few coming from Canada and the United Kingdom.

Archaeological Impact Assessments

Archaeological impact assessments (AIAs) began to be conducted in Belize
in the 1990s, as a result of rapid development associated with the tourism and
agricultural industries, as well as infrastructural improvements conducted by
the Belize government and international investors. AIAs are predominantly
conducted as part of larger environmental impact assessments (EIAs) and are
overseen by both the Belize Institute of Archaeology and the Department of
the Environment.

Like all research projects, the directors of AIAs must acquire permits from
the Institute of Archaeology to conduct the studies required in the area proposed for development. Applications must define the geographical area to be
investigated, the methodology that will be applied in the study, the names
of senior personnel, and a projected timeline for completion of the project.
Unlike research projects, the principal investigators (PIs) of impact assessments are not required to have PhDs, but each must have at least an MA from
an accredited institution. However, if the project will include major excavations
of ancient monuments, then the Institute of Archaeology generally requests
that archaeologists with PhDs be brought in to conduct the work. Following
completion of AIAs, PIs are required to submit reports that detail results of
their work, a description of sites and artifacts identified or recovered by the
project, and recommendations for the mitigation of impacts on any ancient
monument that could be impacted by the proposed development. All reports
are reviewed by IA personnel who then make a final decision on whether the
development project can proceed. If and when sites need to be salvaged, the
cost of all mitigation required by the Institute of Archaeology must be paid for
by the developer. All antiquities recovered by these salvaged projects must also
be handed over to the Institute of Archaeology for curation, and the PI must
submit a monograph-style final report describing the excavations and analyses
of cultural remains recovered by the investigations.

The longest and most intensive mitigation project conducted to date in
Belize was a two-year-long archaeological salvage project in the upper Macal

River Valley. This project was paid for by the Belize Electric Company Limited (BECOL) prior to the construction of a hydroelectric dam in western Belize. The project included the survey of a five-kilometer-long section of the Macal River gorge, followed by the excavations of several sites that were destined to be flooded by the construction of the dam. Other extensive salvage projects have been conducted in association with highway expansion and construction, especially in the southern and western parts of the country. More often, however, salvage projects are smaller in scale, and predominantly associated with the construction of tourist resorts along the coast and on offshore islands.

As in the United States and Europe, the major problem with salvage projects is financing. Developers often try to spend as little as possible on these projects, pressuring archaeologists to expedite their surveys and trying to influence the final assessments of the survey area. For these reasons, the Institute of Archaeology generally sends a staff archaeologist to visit properties that will be developed. The salvage archaeologist is required to accompany the government archaeologist on these reconnaissance trips so that they can both confirm the presence of monuments that can potentially be destroyed by the modern development. This also gives both archaeologists an opportunity to discuss ways to mitigate impacts on archaeological resources, and to determine suitable timelines for completion of the work.

Inventorying Cultural Heritage in Belize

Because of Belize's centralized system of management, the National Institute of Culture and History has the sole responsibility for inventorying all forms of heritage in the country. The resulting data are recorded in both electronic and non-electronic formats and stored at the headquarters of the four branches of NICH. In the case of the Institute of Archaeology, the inventory includes descriptions of sites, their cultural affiliation (e.g., Maya, Spanish, British, etc.), their chronological assignment (when possible), their state of preservation, the type of property in which they are located, and their geographical location (i.e., UTM coordinates). To protect against looting, these data are not accessible to the general public, but archaeologists with research permits can request access to those records within the geographic region where they are working. Presently, the site inventory includes surface and subterranean (cave) sites, plus shipwrecks below the territorial waters of the country. Surface sites include pre-Ceramic features, ancient Maya communities and ceremonial centers, Spanish churches, and various types of British colonial-period buildings such as sugar mills, forts, and lighthouses, plus cemeteries.

The Institute also manages a database for antiquities and other types of cultural heritage. This data set includes description of the objects and information on raw material, place of origin, cultural affiliation, date of manufacturing, state of preservation, and, if featured in a publication, the reference or citation for the object. In cases where an object is on loan to a museum or traveling exhibition, this information is also noted in the catalogue card corresponding to the object.

It was noted above that all antiquities in Belize are the property of the government. Lack of storage and curation space, however, has led the Institute of Archaeology to develop a system of custodianship that allows citizens to keep antiquities in their possession and to display these objects in their homes. The citizen must first request to keep these objects in their possession. Once the request is made, the objects are recorded and registered in the central database of the Institute, and a permit is issued to the citizen with the condition that the objects cannot be altered, modified, given away, loaned, or sold. These permits are generally valid for the lifetime of an individual, but cannot be bequeathed to surviving family members. If the latter want to keep the objects in their possession, they must apply for a new permit to be issued in their name.

Funding Cultural Resource Management in Belize

The National Institute of Culture and History acquires funding for the management of Belize's cultural heritage from two major sources: an annual government subvention, and entrance fees to archaeological parks. The government subvention is provided by the Ministry of Finance, and is part of the recurrent budget of the central government. Entrance fees are collected at archaeological sites that are open to the general public, and from visitors to the Museum of Belize. Instead of going to the central government, these funds are deposited directly to the NICH's account. Other sources of income include the rental of facilities, such as the Bliss Center for the Performing Arts; fees charged for filming or for marriage ceremonies at archaeological parks; and the sale of books, brochures, and souvenirs. Additional funds are sometimes acquired through grants from UNESCO, from foreign embassies (e.g., the U.S. Ambassador's Fund for Cultural Preservation), from the European Union, and from other international institutions. Occasionally, local and multinational companies also contribute funding for specific projects. All funding acquired by NICH is disbursed at the start of the fiscal year to the four branches of the institution. The largest disbursement goes to the Institute of Archaeology, followed by the Institute of Creative Arts, the Museum of Belize, and the Institute of Social and Cultural Research.

CRM in Belize and Central America

While the management of cultural resources in Belize shares some similarities with the systems of its Central American neighbors, there are also some very significant differences. After the passage of the NICH Act in 2000, for example, CRM in Belize became centralized and executed under a single legislation.

NICH is also a quasi-government institution, and operates much like Crown corporations in Canada and the United Kingdom. This allows NICH to engage in business ventures, apply for grants like an NGO, and enter into business agreements with private and foundational co-managers while still affiliated with a central government ministry. NICH is affiliated with the Ministry of Education and Culture, and the president of NICH answers to the minister of government who holds the education and culture portfolio.

Cultural resource management in most of Central America, as in the United States, is neither a unitary nor a centralized system. In some cases, different cultural institutions are spread across several different government ministries, each with its own separate legislation. In other cases, one or more cultural institutions are within similar government ministries, but incorporated in the portfolios of different vice-ministers. In Guatemala, for example, the Instituto de Antropología e Historia (IDAEH), which is responsible for the management of archaeological and historical monuments and objects, is incorporated within the Ministry of Culture and Sports. The Instituto de Bellas Artes (Institute of Fine Arts) is also under the Ministry of Culture and Sports, but headed by its own vice-minister.

In Honduras, management of cultural resources falls under the jurisdiction of the Instituto Hondureño de Antropología e Historia (IDEA). Unlike the heritage management institutions of Belize and Guatemala, IDEA is an autonomous scientific and technical institution with four major departments: the Department of Historical Research, the Department of Museums, the Department for the Protection of Cultural Heritage, and the Restoration Department. As in Belize, IDEA receives some financial support from the central government. Unlike NICH in Belize, however, IDEA has no jurisdiction over music, filming, or the performing arts.

Differences also exist in the heritage legislations of the various Central American nations. In Belize, for example, it is illegal to sell, export, or import antiquities since they are considered the property of the government of Belize or, in the case of importation, the property of a foreign state. In comparison, a citizen in Guatemala can own antiquities but cannot export them. Guatemala also has several private museums that are managed by their respective owners.

Challenges in the Management of Cultural Resources in Belize

The country of Belize has an incredibly rich and diverse intangible cultural heritage, as well as an astonishing number of ancient and historic sites. Archaeological surveys actually indicate that there are still more prehistoric buildings than modern houses and that the largest structures in the country are still ancient pyramids at the Maya sites of Caracol and Xunantunich. While Belizeans are very proud of these impressive cultural statistics, the National

Institute of Culture and History continues to be very concerned with the difficult challenges of protecting and preserving this impressive heritage. In the case of archaeology, this concern remains despite the fact that nearly 50 percent of the total land mass of Belize is under some form of reserve or national park. As with most other Mundo Maya (World of the Maya) countries,[11] the protection of archaeological sites from looting and industrial development remains one of the greatest challenges faced by heritage managers in Belize. This challenge is compounded by the fact that much of the country is underdeveloped, forested, and difficult to access. The poorly patrolled border between Belize and Guatemala also makes it easy for looters to cross the border undetected, and to pillage sites in remote parts of the country.

In the case of intangible heritage, rapid globalization and exposure to Latin American, Caribbean, and North American media and the Internet pose a major challenge to the preservation of native cultural traditions. In recent times, a growing number of younger Belizeans have been exposed to foreign traditions—particularly through music, film, dress, and urban North American lifestyles—and have begun emulating these traditions at the cost of their own. It is for these reasons that the Institutes of Creative Arts and Social and Cultural Research have been recording and promoting the diverse cultural traditions in the country, and working proactively with the Ministry of Education and Culture to bring these traditions to the classrooms.

The four branches of NICH have started to apply other innovative strategies to protect the cultural heritage of the country. These new strategies include partnering with non-governmental institutions, launching various types of cultural educational programs to promote community involvement, job creation, and the ratification of bilateral cultural agreements with neighboring countries. In the case of institutional partnerships, for example, the Institute of Archaeology has joined with several NGOs and the Belize Defence Force to patrol and monitor national parks and sites in remote locations of the country. Whereas in the past the IA provided little input on the location of research projects, it now actively recruits archaeologists to work in remote regions by facilitating permitting procedures for those willing to work at these sites. With regard to education programs, the Institute of Archaeology assists the Ministry of Tourism with its national tour guide training program, and provides documentaries on Belizean heritage for airing on local television stations. The IA has joined the Ministry of Education and Culture in launching a Maya and African studies program for primary, secondary, and tertiary education. The Institute also holds an annual symposium in Belizean archaeology, and publishes the proceedings of the meetings in a journal-style monograph.

In August 2005, the Institute of Archaeology signed a Tri-National Protected Areas and Conservation Memorandum of Understanding (MOU) with Mexico and Guatemala. The purpose of the MOU is to enable international cooperation in the protection, conservation, and sustainable management of natural and cultural resources. In 2012, the Institute of Archaeology signed a bilateral agreement with the United States to impose import restrictions for archaeological and ethnological objects under the 1970 UNESCO Convention on the Means of Prohibiting and Preventing the Illicit Import, Export and Transfer of Ownership of Cultural Property. This agreement was renewed for another five-year term in 2018. Yet another bilateral agreement for the promotion, conservation, and promotion of cultural traditions between Belize and Mexico has been in place for more than a decade.

Locally, Belize continues to successfully integrate tourism and cultural resource management as a way of providing rural communities with economic incentives and as a means to help preserve and protect cultural resources and traditions across the country. Through the restoration of archaeological sites, the creation of museums and visitor centers, the promotion of local arts and crafts, and the dissemination of cultural information, there has been a marked drop in looting and site destruction and a revitalization of cottage industries. Many of the objects produced by the latter industries make their way to the tourist markets, particularly in the rural communities adjacent to heritage sites that have become important tourist destinations. Archaeological salvage projects have also been on the rise, fueled by continued growth and development in the tourism and agricultural sectors. Like all developing countries, however, the lack of financial and human resources remains a major challenge to Belize's ability to manage its rich and diverse cultural heritage. In spite of these challenges, Belize continues to be very proactive in its efforts to monitor and manage development, and to enact sound legislation for protecting and preserving its past for the future.

— • —

A Very Brief Introduction to China's *Wenwu* Management System and CRM Archaeology

Wang Renyu

Quite different from the fragmented CRM system of the United States, China has a rather centralized "top-down" cultural resource management approach, with the National Bureau of Cultural Relics at the top. The Bureau, affiliated with the Cultural Ministry of the People's Republic of China (PRC) Central Government, was formally established in 1949 by the Central People's Government[12] and assigned the responsibility of administering tangible heritage, museums, and libraries at the national level. In 1983, the Advisory Council of

Cultural Relics was established. The members of the Council are mostly specialists with expertise in history, archaeology, and historic buildings research. Their main task is to offer advice to the Bureau on heritage preservation and management, among many other things. Unlike the bureaucratic system of the United States, as the only leading agency in cultural resource management of the Central Government, the Bureau has the power to direct the work of CRM departments in provincial and local governments throughout the country.

Laws and Cultural Property Ownership

In 1982, China's first law on *wenwu*[13] preservation and management was enacted during the twenty-fifth meeting of the Standing Committee of the National People's Congress. Entitled *The Law of the People's Republic of China in the Protection of Cultural Relics*, it has been amended five times, from 1991 through 2017. According to this law, "in the People's Republic of China, any cultural relic ... should be protected by the State. Destruction of it and shipment abroad are prohibited. People's committees at various levels hold responsibility for the protection of cultural relics within their own jurisdiction. All cultural relics left unearthed belong to the State."

Oversight Agencies and Archaeological Resource Preservation Units

The CRM oversight agencies of China include primarily cultural relics departments at all levels of government, including the Central, provincial, and county cultural agencies, and sometimes even those in townships. Apart from the overarching law universally respected by the whole society, the Bureau and sometimes provincial governments also prescribe a host of regulations concerning the protection of important cultural heritage sites, such as the Great Wall and the Maritime Silk Road. China's "cultural relics" in the form of archaeological sites, structures, buildings, and building complexes are usually organized into a three-level preservation unit (*baohu danwei*) system, including heritage sites with local (usually county) significance, provincial significance, and national significance. It is required by the Bureau that provincial and local governments prepare preservation plans for heritage sites of high importance, especially the ones in the Register of Heritage Sites with National Significance (*Quanguo zhongdian wenwu baohu danwei*). Once having been approved by the Bureau and endorsed by governments at the provincial level, the plans are considered to have the same authority as China's other laws. The Bureau, sometimes together with local governments, allocates funds to conserve or maintain archaeological sites or ancient building complexes with significance at various levels.

CRM Archaeology, Great Archaeological Sites, and Archaeological Parks

In the early days of the National Bureau of Cultural Relics, its director co-chaired both the Bureau and the Institute of Archaeology of the Chinese Academy of Social Sciences. Thus, as the leading archaeological research institution, the Institute could provide massive support and useful advice on decision-making procedures dominated by the Bureau. There has been no distinction between academic archaeology and CRM archaeology as there is in the United States. Up to the present, nearly all archaeological work in China has mostly been carried out by non-profit archaeological institutes at various levels, fully funded by the Chinese government and sometimes by archaeology departments in universities. In recent years, for-profit companies have played a more important role in archaeological survey work by using Chinese augers.

In the early twenty-first century, due to the huge pressure caused by China's urban expansion, the National Bureau staff together with archaeologists from the Institute of Archaeology and Peking University selected 200 archaeological sites of top significance from all the then-known sites listed in the Register of Heritage Sites with National Significance; such sites are usually called the Great Archaeological Sites (*Da yizhi*) of China. Because of their unparalleled significance, the Bureau and provincial governments usually pay more attention to these sites and fully sponsor the cost of their conservation, including survey, excavation, and site planning. In 2010, 12 of these sites were designated as National Archaeological Parks (*Guojia kaogu yizhi gongyuan*). In late 2017, 36 Great Archaeological Sites were nominated and subsequently designated as National Archaeological Parks. These initiatives attest to the importance archaeological resource management in China.

— • —

CRM in Europe

Raimund Karl

In Europe, CRM is a multibillion dollar industry, even if only archaeology (which is often treated separately from built heritage) is considered. Much as is to be expected, it is done very similarly to how it is done in the United States in some regards, but quite differently in others. Generally speaking, CRM is considerably more state-controlled in much of Europe than it is in the United States, and tends to allow for much more intervention in private property rights, though the main mechanisms by which it is done—*land and resource management* and *environmental impact assessment* (EIA)—are quite similar.[14]

Democratic (Capitalist) Countries

Where the basics are concerned, most European states these days are democratic countries. The majority are republics, with some constitutional monarchies being the exception, though even in these, political power rests with Parliament, and monarchs are little more than ceremonial heads of state. In some countries (e.g., France, Italy, Austria), CRM is a matter of the national government, while in other countries (e.g., the United Kingdom, Germany) the responsibility falls to the constituent federal states. Like the United States, much of Europe is capitalist—though considerably less fiercely so—resulting in very similar conflicts between private property rights and heritage protection.

Who Owns What?

By and large, most land in Europe is privately owned. However, in contrast to the United States, numerous constraints are placed on land use, especially with regard to development, but to a lesser extent also where other land use—including farming and forestry—are concerned. Particularly in densely built-up areas, like cities, zoning and planning controls may be very restrictive.

In most European countries, heritage management, planning, and other relevant laws apply equally to all land—and any movable property deemed to be cultural heritage—regardless of whether it is privately or publicly owned. Most relevant laws in Europe date from the late nineteenth or early twentieth century and have since (more or less regularly) been adapted to reflect changes in society and economy. Generally speaking, they are mostly concerned with setting constraints on the unrestricted ("free") use of property that is deemed to be or to contain cultural heritage.

In most countries, the responsibility to protect and preserve any cultural heritage falls on the owner of the portable object or immovable property in question, whether it be a private person or public body. However, some countries, like Italy, automatically declare all archaeology of national or regional significance to be the property of the state by law if it is immovable and is located on or underneath the surface of the ground, even though the title of the property itself (upon or under which the cultural heritage exists) is not normally affected. Governments' compulsory purchase of land containing cultural heritage is possible in most European countries if the locally responsible government agency deems acquisition necessary, especially if the land can no longer be used productively by any private owners because of significant cultural heritage being located on or underneath it.

Where Most CRM Work Is Being Done, and by Whom

Generally, CRM work will get carried out in the context of all major developments (normally as defined by either European Union or national law) in the context of pre-development EIAs. Usually, EIA legislation includes a requirement for landowners/developers to fund any CRM work that becomes necessary due to the development. In most European countries, any development will require state consent in the context of land and resource management controls, with any necessary CRM work normally being set as firm conditions in permits. Where specifically protected (e.g., listed, scheduled, etc.) cultural heritage is concerned, any significant change of land use may require a state permit, which can require compliance with quite restrictive conditions, such as the use of permissible farming methods, restrictions on plowing, prohibitions on any digging, and so forth.

Conditions may and will often include a requirement for CRM work to be carried out prior to any changes to the land or land use being made. Almost invariably, any such work must be conducted by qualified CRM professionals, though the precise qualifications required for directing and conducting such works vary somewhat from country to country—and in federally organized countries, sometimes even from state to state.

In addition, in almost all of Europe, most intentional archaeological fieldwork for research purposes (including non-destructive surveys) requires a state permit, regardless of whether the targeted site is specifically protected or whether any cultural heritage is known or suspected to exist there. In most European countries, such permits are issued only sparingly and may, in some, be issued only to persons who hold a relevant university degree. While in most countries, such a requirement will normally apply only to the director of the fieldwork in question (whether it is CRM or "pure" research), in some, it can also apply to some or all fieldwork staff.

Beyond development control and research fieldwork, many state or national heritage agencies also carry out their own fieldwork, with some directly engaged in CRM, and others concentrating their (usually very limited) resources on necessary rescue works unrelated to development control (e.g., naturally eroding sites). Heritage agency staff are often exempt from permit requirements for CRM work carried out on behalf of the state.

In very simplified terms, in Europe, CRM is done whenever it may be required by law and is deemed necessary by the state (represented through its heritage public officials), mostly in, but not limited to, development control. Generally speaking, this is a very good system, though it is not without its problems, especially where funding for CRM works not related to development control is concerned.

Where Does the Money Come From?

Where development-related CRM is concerned, the money in most European states comes primarily from developer funding. In most countries, developer funding works by means of direct contracts between the developer and private archaeological contractors (mostly organized as private companies, trusts, or charities), with the state only setting conditions regarding planning, fieldwork, and so on in relevant permits. In some countries, however, even some or most of developer-funded CRM work is done by state agencies (or wholly or partially state-owned companies or other kinds of organizations), with the developer being charged directly by the state (usually a prearranged sum) for the costs of the works.

In addition to this, many state and/or national governments provide their respective heritage agencies with some (though most often quite limited) funding for supporting directly or grant-funding some (especially small-scale private) development-related CRM or any non-development-related CRM they deem necessary. This funding is partially spent by these agencies on their own work, but it can be and is also at least partially contracted out to private providers in many countries.

Still, the majority of all CRM (and other archaeology-related fieldwork) is also compliance-driven in most European countries these days, and funding is provided by private developers (mostly larger construction companies) by means of the "polluter pays" principle, loosely based on the provisions of the European Convention for the Protection of the Archaeological Heritage (revised).[15] That said, these developers in turn lay the costs they incur for compliance off onto the end users, which often—especially where large-scale infrastructural developments are concerned—is the state, who thus frequently pays for CRM work by proxy (providing a nice additional profit margin to private construction companies). Thus, where this—in theory very good—funding system is concerned, in practice, it may often involve considerably less effective use of public funds than if it were given directly to heritage agencies or CRM providers.

Problems

Given that the general setup and historical development of CRM in Europe is quite similar to that in the United States—though it kicked off with a vengeance about a decade or two later—most of the problems faced are the same as in the United States. Particularly, CRM practitioners are often considered to be "second-rate archaeologists," often not only by university-based academics, but also by archaeologists in public service.

In addition, heritage agencies are often seen—especially, but not exclusively, by developers and landowners—as the "agency that says no," and therefore are not always overly popular. Thus, there quite frequently can be issues with members of the public, especially those who might be adversely affected by the heritage agencies getting involved in "their business," and who, as a result, do not report cultural heritage or indeed actively try to hide the fact that heritage might be affected by their planned activities. CRM contractors and consultants also sometimes face problems with developers who ask them to cut corners or "unfind things" that would complicate development projects, both in EIAs and normal land management. While in Europe, these CRM contractors can oftentimes rely on strong support from relatively powerful state agencies, this support is not necessarily always forthcoming forcefully enough to fully counter client demands to cut corners.

Being state agencies also means that the "watchdogs" can and often are subject to—sometimes immense—political pressure as well as economic lobbying by political proxy. Thus, while in theory, the state agencies are often quite powerful, in practice they are sometimes as powerless as the CRM contractor in their dealings with at least some clients.

Community Engagement

While virtually all European states increasingly strongly encourage community involvement in and engagement with cultural heritage, including especially through the Council of Europe Framework Convention on the Value of Cultural Heritage for Society,[16] as yet there is only very limited public involvement in CRM in most of Europe. This is mostly due to a combination of limitations imposed by CRM processes, but also partially due to professional reservations against public involvement. The latter is usually justified by arguments relating to archaeological quality assurance; however, this at least partially appears to be a smokescreen to hide fears of losing jobs in the sector to "untrained" members of the public doing "the same work for free." Combined with fears (partially justified, but most often irrational) that archaeology may fall victim to looters, some state agencies even keep their registers of known archaeological sites secret and actively hide some CRM work from the public, at least until it has been fully completed. Thus, while in theory CRM should involve quite a lot of community engagement in much of Europe, in practice that commitment exists more on paper than in reality.

Regulators

In much of Europe, the regulators are state agencies, with highly variable remits and duties]. Most CRM archaeologists will normally deal directly either with state heritage agency officials, most of whom are archaeology graduates, or with planning control officers, who sometimes are archaeology graduates as well, but more often are not. It is these people who normally set the conditions for CRM work and control compliance. Reports produced during the CRM work are usually sent to them.

Especially if they are state agency archaeologists, regulators may make more or less regular site visits while the work is being carried out for quality control purposes. They may also reserve the right to interfere with on-site decisions regarding work carried out by the CRM archaeologist (or company) at the site. Such interference rights may include decisions concerning fieldwork strategy, but they can go as far in some cases as to include the right to request the removal of particular staff members from the project team. In some countries, it is these officers who have the authority to "clear" projects before or after any necessary CRM work has been completed and any reports have been filed with them. In other countries, they themselves report to a higher authority within their respective bureaucracies, which can be a higher-ranking professional within the state agency, or a political body like a planning board.

What CRM Archaeologists Do

In much of Europe, consultation with developers and landowners, as well as most of the background research and scoping, is done by state or national heritage agencies themselves, though they have increasingly started to contract out these parts of their jobs, mostly due to understaffing. In many countries, CRM archaeologists in the "private" or "commercial" sector mostly do the actual fieldwork and report writing—assessing and resolving the adverse effects on cultural heritage of development and other "threats" to its long-term preservation—that are necessary as part of compliance with permit conditions, though in some states even that still is mostly done by state agencies or companies. The actual work done, whether by state agency officials or private archaeological contractors, is mostly identical to what is done in the United States.

In most of Europe, evaluation of cultural heritage is one of the main tasks of state or national heritage agencies, and is mostly or exclusively done by these agencies themselves. Only some heritage agencies in Europe have publicly communicated the criteria they use for determining the value and/or significance of cultural heritage, with some not even having any predetermined criteria that they consistently apply.

Quite often, all different types of cultural heritage are referred to (at least in professional jargon and law) by catch-all terms like "monuments," with the term usually referring to tangible heritage evaluated to be sufficiently significant to merit at least some degree of protection by the state. While particularly ("nationally" or "regionally," sometimes even only "locally") significant "monuments" are usually "listed" in some kind of register, requiring their owners to preserve them indefinitely *in situ* (mostly) unchanged and usually at their own expense, most other "monuments" are also protected (though considerably less strongly) through the planning process in most European countries. Of course, background research and fieldwork reports written by "commercial" CRM archaeologists may and often will contain statements about the value and/or significance of any "historical" objects, buildings, sites, or wider areas like landscapes. But these assessments in most European states are considered at best to be advice from the heritage agencies, and at worst are disregarded altogether.

Where "portable antiquities" are concerned, many European states claim ownership under "treasure trove" legislation for finds that are deemed to be cultural heritage, or at least that upon evaluation are considered "significant" portable objects. Where professional CRM work is concerned, any finds made and any records created must usually be deposited in some public archaeological archive or in a public museum collection, whether by law or by permit condition. As a result of this, in many European countries there is an increasingly acute problem with suitable space for archaeological archiving: the archives of some state heritage agencies contain—literally—tens of millions of finds, with storage space running out more quickly than new space can be acquired with the available funds. This can have a considerable indirect effect on CRM companies, who may not always be able to find suitable archives to deposit the evidence they collect during fieldwork.

— • —

CRM in Nigeria

Kolawole Adekola

Cultural resource management barely exists in Nigeria. In fact, in terms of the picture painted by this book, one can confidently assert that CRM is not a feature of the Nigerian landscape.

In Nigeria, attention is hardly given to likely effects on cultural resources by any agencies, whether large or small, that deal with land. Ministries dealing with large portions of land at the federal level are many: Power, Housing, and Works; Petroleum Resources; Agriculture; Federal Capital Territory; Aviation; Defense; Commerce and Tourism; Transportation; Health and Social Services; Education; Youth and Sports; Internal Affairs; Water Resources; Solid Minerals Development; Information and Culture; Justice; and Communications. Other ministries, such as Finance, Economic Development, and Environment, deal with large expanses of land as well, but the scale is not as enormous as those just mentioned, particularly the first twelve. As of today, none of these ministries has a unit to perform archaeological impact assessment prior to project execution. They are also not compelled by any regulations to consult archaeologists or cultural resource managers in the course of their respective projects. Consequently, large plots of land are bulldozed daily in the construction of highways, housing estates, refineries and other hydrocarbon facilities, airports, mechanized agricultural farms, prison yards, borders, schools (primary, secondary, and universities), hospitals (teaching hospitals, primary health centers, and other health-related facilities), military barracks (army, naval, air force, and police), industrial estates, and so on. Each of these ministries embarks on construction works that cover several hectares of land with no record of appraisal of such land by archaeologists.

The laws in Nigeria covering cultural resources are mainly general laws. They do not address specific needs that could encourage the practice of CRM. The laws are also obsolete. The last time a workshop was held on the review of the Nigerian antiquities law was 6 October 2011. Several portions of the Nigerian cultural statues of 1979 need to be reviewed to meet the challenges of the twenty-first century.

Secondly, archaeology itself has yet to be liberalized in Nigeria. As of today, it is practiced mainly as a government-controlled operation, with practitioners mainly working for the government via academia and museums. The biggest employer of archaeologists ordinarily ought to be the National Commission for Museums and Monuments, the agency saddled with the protection of Nigerian cultural resources. The Commission has museums in major centers all over the federation, but as of today the total number of archaeologists on its wage bill is less than thirty. The situation in the universities is no better: there are only six universities with full-fledged archaeology departments. Four of the universities are owned by the federal government, while the other two are owned by state governments. Nigeria is a country with 36 states plus a seat of government known as the Federal Capital Territory. The population of the country is around 198 million, but this is a conservative estimate as the last population census was held in Nigeria in 2006 and the population of the country then was 140,431,790 according to the National Population Commission, the agency saddled with the population census.

Of the four universities owned by the federal government, only two have more than 10 archaeologists on staff, while the state universities have staff strength of less than 5 each. At the time of this writing, there are 10 archaeologists at the University of Ibadan.

Today in Nigeria, many graduates of archaeology at first degree and master's degree levels serve in several other capacities, since there are no avenues for practicing archaeology. Some use the study of archaeology as a springboard to qualify for basic training in other professions. Consequently, many brilliant young men and women go into other areas of endeavor to earn their daily wages.

Archaeology could be having a boom, had the ministries, departments, and agencies been mandated to have practicing archaeologists on their wage bill.

Had this been the case, many graduates in archaeology could be practicing, and issues of unemployment for graduates in the discipline would not have arisen. The number of graduates produced annually by the various universities would not have been sufficient to meet the needs at the various levels. Archaeology in Nigeria is grossly underfunded.

The only CRM work done by a practicing archaeologist in Nigeria that I know of was carried out in 2014 in Benin, Edo State. The work was contracted to a very senior Nigerian archaeologist by a firm following the construction of a power station. The archaeological impact assessment was done, and the report was delivered to the contracting firm. The client appears to have been a foreign firm. I suspect such projects could have been carried out in the past (either by locals or foreigners), but it may be difficult to find a record of them. Such technical reports are not made public or available even to the archaeology community. In 2015, some indigenous residents of Badagry in Lagos State approached a colleague and me to do similar work for them. This project has not yet materialized as a result of funding and logistics problems.

Contributors

Kolawole Adekola is an archaeologist at the University of Ibadan, Nigeria. He serves on the board of the World Archaeological Congress (WAC) and was formerly on the executive board of the Society of Africanist Archaeologists (SAFA). E-mail: kolawole.adekola@gmail.com

Caitlin Allen is a historical archaeologist and heritage specialist based at the University of Sydney, Australia. She has a particular interest in understanding the ways people make meaning from the past in their everyday lives and how heritage managers can best respond to these meanings in practice. E-mail: caitlin.allen@sydney.edu.au

Jaime J. Awe is an Associate Professor in Anthropology at Northern Arizona University, the Director of the Belize Valley Archaeological Reconnaissance Project (BVAR), and an Emeritus member of the Belize Institute of Archaeology. E-mail: jaime.awe@nau.edu

Raimund Karl is a Professor of Archaeology and Heritage at Bangor University in Wales. Archaeological heritage management is one of his main research interests, concentrating on Central Europe. E-mail: r.karl@bangor.ac.uk and see https://archdenk.blogspot.com/

Wang Renyu works for the Institute of Archaeology of the Chinese Academy of Social Sciences as an archaeological resource planner, and has participated in many site preservation and policy-making projects. E-mail: wang.renyu.1978@aliyun.com

Notes

1. See Richard Mackay, "Could Do It Better: An Indigenous Heritage Report Card," AIATSIS Occasional Seminar, 14 May 2014, Canberra ACT, https://aiatsis.gov.au/gallery/video/could-do-it-better-indigenous-heritage-report-card.
2. For more on the development and impact of the Charter, see Australia ICOMOS (International Charter on Monuments and Sites), *Collaboration for Conservation: A Brief History of Australia ICOMOS and the Burra Charter* (Burwood, Victoria: Australia ICOMOS 2016).
3. One issue that can arise from the listing process is that significance assessments often become locked and inflexible to change over time. The system doesn't deal well with the mutable nature of heritage significance.
4. See Sandra Bowdler, "Archaeological Significance as a Mutable Quality," in *Site Surveys and Significance Assessment in Australian Archaeology: Proceedings of the 1981 Springwood Conference on Australian Prehistory*, ed. Sandra Bowdler and Sharon Sullivan (Canberra: Australian National University Press, 1984), 1–9.
5. There are a number of articles on this subject, but the following provide good overviews of the key issues regarding outcomes in both Indigenous and historic archaeological work in Australia over the last 30 years or so: Steve Brown, "Mute or Mutable? Archaeological Significance, Research and Cultural Heritage Management in Australia," *Australian Archaeology* 67 (1) (2008): 19–30; and Siobhán Lavelle, "Archaeology Down Under: Management and Outcomes in the First State in Australia," in *Urban Archaeology, Municipal Government and Local Planning: Preserving Heritage within the Commonwealth of Nations and the United States*, ed. Sherene Baugher, Douglas R. Appler, and William Moss (New York: Springer, 2017), 137–160.
6. See the 2012 report *Comparing the NSW Aboriginal Heritage System with Other Australian Systems*, prepared by the state of NSW and the Office of Environment and Heritage, Sydney, https://www.environment.nsw.gov.au/-/media/OEH/Corporate-Site/Documents/Aboriginal-cultural-heritage/comparing-nsw-aboriginal-heritage-system-with-other-australian-systems-120402.pdf.
7. For more on this subject, see Tracy Ireland and Sandy Blair, "The Future for Heritage Practice," *Historic Environment* 27 (2) (2015): 9–17; and Caitlin Allen, "The Road From Burra: Thoughts on Using the Charter in the Future," *Historic Environment* 18 (1) (2004): 50–53.
8. See the 2010 report *Aboriginal Cultural Heritage Requirements for Proponents*, prepared by the state of NSW and the Office of Environment and Heritage, Sydney, http://alc.org.au/media/43239/1004%20deccw%20community%20consultation%20requirements.pdf.
9. For an example, see Daryle Rigney, Simone Bignall, and Steve Hemming, "Negotiating Indigenous Modernity: Kungun Ngarrindjeri Yunnan—Listen to Ngarrindjeri Speak," *AlterNative* 11 (4) (2015): 334–349.
10. For example, the Byron Shire Council's "Community-Based Heritage Study" was adopted in 2008. See https://www.byron.nsw.gov.au/Services/Building-development/Heritage/Community-Based-Heritage-Study. Guidelines for completing community-based heritage studies can be found at http://www.environment.nsw.gov.au/resources/heritagebranch/heritage/20130215hertagestudy.pdf.
11. See the Mundo Maya website at http://www.mundomaya.travel/.

12. See https://en.wikipedia.org/wiki/National_Cultural_Heritage_Administration.
13. The two-character term *wenwu* (lit., "cultural objects") is used to denote physical cultural resources, that is, tangible cultural heritage, covering historic and archeological sites, structures, groups of buildings, and artifacts. Intangible heritage is usually not deemed as *wenwu* and therefore usually assigned to other departments of the Cultural Ministry.
14. See, for example, the European Union's directive on EIAs: Directive 2014/52/EU, https://eur-lex.europa.eu/legal-content/EN/TXT/PDF/?uri=CELEX:32014L0052 &from=EN.
15. More commonly referred to as the Valletta Convention. See Council of Europe, European Convention on the Protection of the Archaeological Heritage (Revised), La Valletta, 16 January 1992, https://www.coe.int/en/web/culture-and-heritage/ valletta-convention.
16. More commonly referred to as the Faro Convention. See the Council of Europe Framework Convention on the Value of Cultural Heritage for Society, Faro, 27 October 2005, https://www.coe.int/en/web/conventions/full-list/-/conventions/ rms/0900001680083746).

Chapter 9

Thoughts in Conclusion

Some Bottom Lines

I hope reading this book has persuaded you of at least the following:

1. CRM is—or at least can and should be—more than archaeology. It's arguably a kind of applied cultural anthropology, but it's also its own, interdisciplinary thing, to which archaeology, ethnography, history, architecture, and many other fields contribute. If you're going to work in the field, you'll do well to know enough about all those non-archaeological disciplines at least to recognize when you need help, and know how to find it.
2. In CRM as in other endeavors, it's important to *question the experts*—within disciplines and across them—notably including experts anointed as such by government authority.
3. CRM does not guarantee the preservation of anything—archaeological sites, valued landscapes, historic buildings, languages, cultural traditions—but it *should* ensure that their preservation is respectfully considered, integrated into planning, and weighed and balanced in management along with economic and non-cultural environmental costs and benefits.
4. CRM is fundamentally about working with people and communities. Its main purposes are to ensure that the heritage values held dear by people and communities are respected by government and industry, to manage wisely those cultural resources over which government has control or influence, and to encourage similar management of such resources outside government's reach.
5. CRM is not easy, intellectually or otherwise. It requires you to know about a wide range of topics—many of them unpredictable until you encounter them— and to work respectfully with a mix of people, enterprises, and interests.
6. You will be very well served in CRM by developing people skills. You will be forever dealing with a variety of people and points of view. Being openminded, willing to listen actively, able to ask questions respectfully, and prepared to pay attention to, and if possible act on, what people tell you—all these attributes will help you do a good job in CRM.

A Future for CRM?

Some of my colleagues have encouraged me to say something about how CRM in the United States should be rebuilt once the current winter of our national discontent is behind us (assuming we survive it). I don't think I can do better than to quote Henry David Thoreau: "Our life is frittered away by detail … Simplicity, simplicity, simplicity!"[1]

CRM in the United States—as I think this book shows—has become monstrously complicated. Most of us fritter away our professional lives enmeshed in details: pseudo-academic arguments about which evaluation criteria or criteria of adverse effect apply, or whether we should call something "avoidance" or "reduction" or "mitigation."

Despite all the detail, CRM in the United States lacks a clearly stated central principle; indeed, even the subject is ill-defined. Is it the same as "historic preservation"? Is it more? Less? Different? Does it even exist? If it does, what is it?

I have the strange notion that cultural resource management ought to involve the management of cultural resources, but none of the cat's cradle of legal authorities with which we wrestle actually says that. Each deals with only a piece of the puzzle. As a result, it's easy enough just to do archaeology or architectural history or historical architecture and say you're doing CRM. And in a way you are; you're just not doing it *all*. And there's no easy way for ordinary people—the people affected by your actions, and who pay for your work—to know that you're doing something less.

Whatever we're doing, it's easy to get wrapped up in the minutiae of doing it, at the expense of accomplishing anything real, let alone anything understandable by the people whose tax dollars and fees support CRM's institutions. As the system stands today, Minutiae R Us.

So if I could, this is what I'd do—again, *in the United States*. It's quite outside my portfolio to offer prescriptions to others. I'd enact a simple law obligating the federal government and those it assists and licenses to respect the cultural heritage of the nation's people, including its tribes, communities, regions, and groups, by

- identifying those aspects of cultural heritage—physical and intangible—that may be affected by any contemplated action, whether directly, indirectly, or as part of a pattern of cumulative effects; and
- seeking ways to avoid, minimize, or otherwise mitigate adverse effects in ways that respect heritage values;
- all in respectful consultation with everyone who may be affected.

That's it. Do away with the National Register of Historic Places (NRHP), or retain it as a quaint honorific institution without planning implications, and do away with NHPA Section 106 review as it's practiced today, with all its nitpicky twists and turns.

If that big a purge isn't feasible, the next best thing would be to keep Section 106 more or less as it is, but uncouple it from the NRHP. Claudia Nissley and I have published a short paper about how to do this,[2] which has been politely ignored by the official CRM community.

If even *that* sort of decoupling isn't possible, the *next* best thing would be to force the National Park Service—and it would take very forceful forcing—to rethink the directions it gives about how eligibility for the NRHP must be determined.

For example, going back to the hypothetical bridge discussed in chapter 5, suppose you go out to inspect the project's APE and notice that the rural side of the inlet is an agricultural landscape in which people are operating family farms pretty much as they have since the eighteenth or nineteenth century. Sure, they're using tractors rather than oxen, and most of them live in relatively modern houses, but in essence they're using the land as they have for many generations. A little consultation with the farm families convinces you that a lot of them would like things to stay that way.

You ought, I think, to be able to write up a report saying that the area at the rural end of the proposed bridge looks like it's a cultural landscape or rural historic district that's eligible for the NRHP, and get on to consulting about what effects the bridge will have and what to do about them. The NHPA Section 106 regulations permit this, but they don't *mandate* it, and the chances are very good that you'll be told by the SHPO, or by your boss based on her or his reading of NRHP guidance, that anything so intuitively rational is forbidden. Instead, you're likely to be told to go research the history, archaeology, and architecture of each farmstead so as to figure out which ones do and don't "contribute" to the landscape, and document the results in a report or on standard forms. If, as I usually am, you're working for local citizens or tribes, you and your clients probably don't have the money to do all that. If you're working for a government agency or the project proponent, your client is likely to say, "We don't *want* to do all that. Let's just look at direct physical impacts on specific archaeological sites and old buildings." If they have enough clout, your clients may be able to make that stick. At which point the only recourse for people who'd like to see the landscape given fair consideration is to go to court, at great cost to all concerned and with no certain outcome.

It's an absurd situation that we ought to correct. One way or another, we ought to stop sweating the small stuff and create a simple system that citizens can understand and that allows us to identify and deal with impacts on the cultural resources that people really care about.

I hear the obvious criticism. To make any such simple system work, and not be abused, it would be necessary to have a regulatory regime, and we'd soon be right back to nitpicking technical minutiae pretty much as we are today. That may be true, but it doesn't have to be. Yes, there would need to be a regulatory regime. Yes, there would have to be carrots for compliance and sticks for non-compliance. But surely we could construct such a regime and gather such sticks and carrots in ways that would result in something more sensible than what we have today. We'll never know if we don't try.

I said I wouldn't presume to speak to the CRM systems employed by other countries, and I won't, but I have to say that in building a new system for the United States, I would not emulate the highly governmental systems described by some of the contributors to chapter 8. There is strength and simplicity in vesting all authority and responsibility in government agencies, but such a system, I think, is inherently conservative and will inevitably evolve toward self-preservation at the expense of its statutory mission, to say nothing of the public interest. I think I would opt instead—if I could—for a non-centralized regime, having recourse to clear, binding regulations and some sort of mandatory advisory oversight. Not entirely unlike what the ACHP is supposed to provide in the United States today, but more thoughtfully constructed and responsibly administered.

For somewhat similar reasons, I would not push for public ownership of all "cultural resources" or even all "antiquities," as is the case in countries like China and some Latin American and European nations—however shocking the chicken grit example I posited in the introduction may have been to my friends there. There is a substantial book to be written about how and why such systems don't work very well (I recommend the writings of Raimund Karl on this subject[3]), but if nothing else, I'd argue that private property rights in the United States are themselves, to many citizens, a treasured cultural resource.

All this said, it would be fascinating and challenging, and maybe even rewarding, to try to design a new CRM system for the United States—one that *actually manages* cultural resources and the impacts of the modern world on them. But I'm afraid that at this point it would be a highly hypothetical exercise; no one in authority seems much interested. At best, assuming we get through the next few years more or less intact, I expect we'll continue to muddle through with CRM as we do now. So my best advice is to learn how to muddle, and try to muddle in a manner that shows respect for the past and responsibility toward the present and future. Without taking yourself or the system too terribly seriously.

Acknowledgments

This book has benefited immeasurably from the contributions of my several collaborators, listed on the title page, and of course from those who provided specific papers for chapter 8. To all these colleagues, I owe a great debt of thanks. I am also grateful for input from Shelly Davis-King, Claudia Nissley, and Judy Scott Feldman. I deeply appreciate the support of all those who've helped in our rather ragged run to publication, including Eliot Werner, Robert Bettinger, Gary Feinman, Wesley Furlong, Wendi Schnaufer, Mitch Allen, Caryn Berg, Elizabeth Martinez, and Shawn Kendrick. For the cover art I'm indebted to the photographic prowess and generosity of Scott Hess.

Notes

1. Henry David Thoreau, Walden (Princeton, NJ: Princeton University Press, [1854] 2004). See also https://www.goodreads.com/quotes/897002-our-life-is-frittered-away-by-detail-simplicity-simplicity-simplicity-i.
2. Claudia Nissley and Thomas F. King, "Simplifying Section 106 Review: A Proposal for 'Streamlining' a Complex Part of Environmental Impact Assessment," *Environmental Practice* 19(2) (2017): 80–83.
3. Cf. Raimund Karl, "Judgement Day in Heritage Hell: Heritage Practice, Policy, and the Law in Austria (and Beyond)," *Historic Environment Policy & Practice* 9(2) (2018): 128–149.

Appendix
Legal Matters

Basics: Treaties, Laws, Regulations, Guidelines, Standards, etc.

CRM is practiced with reference to a variety of legal provisions, including (but not limited to) treaties, laws, regulations, guidelines, and standards. Generally, the following apply:

- A *treaty* is an agreement between two sovereign governments, or among multiple such governments. In the United States, treaties are said to be "the supreme law of the land," superior even to the provisions of the United States Constitution. This is what gives treaties executed by the United States government with Indian tribes their particular force. United Nations *declarations* are treaty-like international agreements subscribed to by all or most or many member nations. *Conventions* issued by organizations like UNESCO (United Nations Educational, Scientific and Cultural Organization) are also treaty-like, being (in theory) binding on those nations that agree to them.

- A *law* is an instrument enacted by some government's ruling body. It is binding either on everyone within that government's jurisdiction or on specified parties. In the United States, a federal law is a federal law only when it's enacted by the United States Congress and signed by the president, or enacted by Congress over the president's veto. *Decrees* and *orders*—in the United States, *executive orders*—are issued by heads of government and in some cases have the force of law. In the United States, executive orders issued by the president or the governor of a state must be grounded in a law or laws. They generally are directions to government agencies about how a law or group of laws should be implemented.

- A *regulation* is promulgated by some government agency that is authorized by statute to do so (in the United States, this is called having "rulemaking authority"). A regulation usually has the force of law because it is issued "pursuant to"—that is, authorized by—some law.

- A *guideline* is a recommendation. In the United States, it is common for agencies responsible for programs to issue guidelines about how those programs should work, or how regulations should be interpreted. A guideline does not have the force of law, but constitutes the relevant agency's advice about best practices. International organizations like UNESCO also issue guidelines; in UNESCO's case these are usually cast as *recommendations* to participating national governments.

- A *standard* is kind of midway between a regulation and a guideline. It doesn't have the force of law, but it's issued by a government agency with reference to something about which the agency is thought to be expert, and others are more or less expected to comply with it.

There are many other forms of government direction/guidance, and it is not uncommon for the least definitive of these—for example, guidelines and standards—to become so set in practice that, for all practical purposes, they become laws.

Some Key International Declarations/Conventions

- **The United Nations Declaration on the Rights of Indigenous Peoples** (UNDRIP) establishes principles by which signatory nations are supposed to be guided in dealing with indigenous populations. Among the most directive, and controversial, of these is the right of indigenous people to give or withhold "free, prior, and informed consent" (FPIC) to projects that may affect them or their territories. Of course, there is a lot of room for disagreement about what each of these words means (except perhaps "and"). See https://en.unesco.org/indigenous-peoples/undrip.

- **The World Heritage Convention** (WHC) is a UNESCO convention, binding on its signatories, that creates the World Heritage List—a list of places of ostensible "outstanding universal value" for their cultural or natural qualities. Various international organizations provide grants and technical assistance for the management of such places. See http://whc.unesco.org/en/convention/.

- **The Convention for the Safeguarding of the Intangible Cultural Heritage** is another UNESCO convention, modeled on the WHC, that lists "intangible" cultural resources thought to have outstanding importance. See https://ich.unesco.org/en/convention#art2.

There are a number of other international conventions and recommendations that deal with aspects of cultural heritage. For information, see https://www.peacepalacelibrary.nl/research-guides/special-topics/cultural-heritage/.

Some Key United States CRM Laws and Regulations

- **The National Environmental Policy Act** (NEPA) establishes United States national policy that favors taking care of the environment, including its cultural aspects. Section 101 lays out general policies, giving the law its name. Section 102 is more procedural; at Section 102(c), NEPA requires federal government agencies to prepare "statements" as to the potential environmental impacts of "major federal actions" they propose to undertake. Extensive regulations issued by the Council on Environmental Quality (CEQ) in the Executive Office of the president specify when and how such statements are to be prepared, reviewed, finalized, and considered in decision making. These include procedures for *categorically excluding* types of action from review, and for the conduct of *environmental assessments* (EA) to determine whether a given proposal is one that requires preparation of an *environmental impact statement* (EIS). The results of project review under NEPA—intended to lay out what the environmental impacts of a project may be—are in theory considered by the relevant federal agency in deciding whether and how to proceed with the project. You can access a summary of the NEPA and download a full text copy at https://energy.gov/nepa/downloads/national-environmental-policy-act-1969. You can download the CEQ regulations, 40 CFR 1500-1508, at https://energy.gov/sites/prod/files/NEPA-40CFR1500_1508.pdf, and access a citizen's guide at https://www.energy.gov/nepa/downloads/citizens-guide-nepa-having-your-voice-heard-ceq-2007.

- **The National Historic Preservation Act** (NHPA) establishes national policy promoting the preservation of "historic properties," defined as places included in or eligible for the National Register of Historic Places (NRHP). It lodged the NRHP in the Department of the Interior, and created the Advisory Council on Historic Preservation (ACHP) as an independent federal agency. It has the Department of the Interior provide grants to states and Indian tribes in order to maintain State and Tribal Historic Preservation Officers (SHPOs/THPOs). At Section 106, the NHPA requires federal agencies to "take into account" the potential effects of their proposed actions on historic properties.

ACHP regulations specify how effects are to be taken into account. These regulations are binding on all United States government agencies. At Section 110, the NHPA outlines additional federal agency responsibilities. Section 101(d)(6) includes requirements for consultation with Indian tribes and Native Hawaiian groups. Section 402 outlines some international responsibilities of the United States government. You can access the text of the NHPA at https://www.nps. gov/history/local-law/nhpa1966.htm. Note that the United States Code (USC) citations have recently changed, but the texts remain the same as when enacted. You can access the ACHP regulations at https://www.law.cornell.edu/cfr/text/36/part-800, and a citizen's guide at https://www.achp.gov/sites/default/files/documents/2017 -01/CitizenGuide.pdf.

- **The Native American Graves Protection and Repatriation Act** (NAGPRA) establishes that Native American ancestral human remains and cultural items belong to the tribes and groups with whose ancestors they are associated, and must be inventoried and returned to federally recognized tribes and Native Hawaiian organizations, both by United States government agencies and by museums that receive United States government assistance. The NAGPRA also provides for the handling of ancestral graves and cultural items found on federal or Indian tribal land. The National Park Service (NPS) has rulemaking authority under the NAGPRA. You can access the text of the NAGPRA at https://www.nps.gov/history/local-law/FHPL_NAG-PRA.pdf, and the NPS regulations (43 CFR 10) at https://www.ecfr. gov/cgi-bin/text-idx?SID=f20968dd90bc649881de8fc3f40cb49e&mc =true&node=pt43.1.10&rgn=div5.

Visit https://www.nps.gov/subjects/historicpreservation/laws-intro.htm for more information on United States historic preservation laws and regulations.

About the Author and Collaborators

Thomas F. King has worked in and around cultural resource management in the United States and Pacific Islands since the 1960s, and is the author of several textbooks on aspects of CRM policy and practice. E-mail: tomking106@gmail.com

Kolawole Adekola is an archaeologist in the Department of Archaeology and Anthropology, University of Ibadan, Nigeria. He is the Junior Representative for the West African Region on the board of the World Archaeological Congress (WAC) and was formerly on the executive board of the Society of Africanist Archaeologists (SAFA). E-mail: kolawole.adekola@gmail.com

Caitlin Allen is a historical archaeologist and heritage specialist based at the University of Sydney, Australia. She has a particular interest in understanding the ways people make meaning from the past in their everyday lives and how heritage managers can best respond to these meanings in practice. E-mail: caitlin.allen@sydney.edu.au

Jaime J. Awe is an Associate Professor in Anthropology at Northern Arizona University, the Director of the Belize Valley Archaeological Reconnaissance Project (BVAR), and an Emeritus member of the Belize Institute of Archaeology. E-mail: jaime.awe@nau.edu

Jaime Lynn Bach is a cultural anthropologist based in Florida, with extensive research experience in Kiribati, and holds a PhD from the University of Montana. As of 2019, she is doing cultural resource management archaeology and ethnography throughout North America. E-mail: jaimelynnbach@gmail.com

Katherine Bracken Ward is a cultural resource archaeologist and paleoethnobotanist who has worked in southern California's Mojave Desert for over 20 years. She also teaches anthropology and operates a community learning center on people-plant relationships in climatically marginal environments. E-mail: katheward@gmail.com

Nancy Farrell is an archaeologist who has engaged in cultural resource management for almost 50 years, primarily in California, Hawaii, and Micronesia. E-mail: nancy@crms.com

Jay W. Gray has worked as a cultural resource management archaeologist in the southern and southeastern United States for more than 20 years. See http://crai-ky.com/staff/jay-gray/

Rebecca A. Hawkins has worked as a cultural resource management archaeologist nationwide for nearly 40 years and co-owns the American Indian-owned Algonquin Consultants, Inc. E-mail: RAHawkins@algonquinconsultants.com

Dawn Johnson is a cultural resource archaeologist specializing in pre-European Northern California. She also has 12 years experience in aviation archaeology in Europe and the Pacific, and has served as a member of The International Group for Historic Aircraft Recovery (TIGHAR)'s Executive Board. E-mail: dawnjhnsn@yahoo.com

Raimund Karl is a Professor of Archaeology and Heritage at Bangor University in Wales. Archaeological heritage management is one of his main research interests, concentrating on Central Europe. E-mail: r.karl@bangor.ac.uk and see https://archdenk.blogspot.com/

Hannah Mattson is a United States Southwest archaeologist and an Assistant Professor of Anthropology at the University of New Mexico. She has over 15 years of experience supervising cultural resource management projects in the southwestern U.S., and works towards incorporating CRM issues and training into academic contexts. E-mail: hmattson@unm.edu

Fred L. McGhee is an African-American archaeologist and activist, based in Austin, Texas. He is the first African-American to graduate from the University of Texas with a PhD in archaeology, and in 2002 he founded the first African-American owned and operated CRM firm. E-mail: fmcghee@flma.org

Jason Nez, an enrolled member of the Navajo Nation, is an archaeologist who specializes in protecting tribal cultural landscapes and traditional places. He has been active in efforts to protect sites that are important in the cultural traditions of the Navajo and other tribes and pueblos—such as the confluence of the Colorado and Little Colorado Rivers—from inappropriate development. E-mail: jmn6@yahoo.com

Wang Renyu works for the Institute of Archaeology of the Chinese Academy of Social Sciences as an archaeological resource planner, and has participated in many site preservation and policy-making projects. E-mail: wang.renyu.1978@aliyun.com

Index

Aboriginal, 116, 136n6, 136n8
Aboriginal Heritage Impact Permit (New South Wales), 116
Academic
    Credentials (BA, MA, PhD), 6, 119–20
    Institutions, 5–6, 90, 94, 112, 123
Advisory Council of Cultural Relics (China), 125–26
Advisory Council on Historic Preservation (ACHP, United States), xiv, 13–17, 25, 72, 75–76, 80–82, 84–85, 102, 141, 145–46
    Comments by, 84–85
Africa(n), 2, 117, 124, 135
African-American, 9, 76
Agencies of government
    Australia, 112, 114–15
    Belize, 117–21
    China, 126
    Europe, 129–133
    Nigeria, 133–34
    United States, xii–xiv, 2–3, 5–6, 8, 13–15, 17–18, 24–31, 36, 41, 45, 48, 54, 58, 62–63, 69–71, 75–81, 83–85, 87–95, 99, 102–4, 106, 112, 115, 140–41, 143–4
Agency for International Development, xv
Agreement, 25–26, 55, 71, 77–82, 84–86, 93, 95, 97–99, 108, 123–25, 143–44
    Memorandum of (MOA, under NHPA Section 106), 79, 81–86, 93, 95
    Non-Disclosure (NDA), 97–99
    Programmatic (PA), 85n1
Agriculture, United States Department of (USDA), xii, 87
Air Force (United States), 87
Alaska, vii, 9, 58, 76, 103
    Native Claims Settlement Act, xii
    Native group, 76

Alternatives, 74, 78, 97, 99, 107
Amazon rainforest, 59n7
America
    Central, 117, 122–23
    Latin, 85, 124, 141
    North, 2, 124
    South, 2
American Cultural Resources Association (ACRA), 22, 109
American Samoa, 13
Anglo-American, 9
Animals, 4, 18, 36, 46, 49, 54, 60, 89, 98
Anthropology, cultural, 5, 8–11, 138
Antiquities, 119–23, 133–34, 141, 143
    Portable, 54, 119, 128, 133
Appalachia, 9
Appendix C to 33 CFR 325, 15
Archaeological
    Data Preservation Act, 2
    Conservancy, 104, 107n5
    And Historic Preservation Act (AHPA), 2
    Impact Assessment (AIA, Belize), 120
    Resources Protection Act (ARPA), 2
Archaeologist(s), archaeology, ix, xiv, xiii, 1–4, 6–16, 18, 28–29, 32, 34–36, 42–44, 49–52, 55–56, 66, 73–74, 79, 87, 92, 95–97, 102–3, 112–14, 116, 120–21, 124, 127, 130–32, 134–35
    Second-rate, 6, 9, 130
Architect(ure), 5, 7, 20, 26, 29, 31, 36, 40, 42, 44, 50–51, 53, 55, 66–67, 69, 92, 96, 101, 112, 138–40
    Classical Revival, 50
    Historical, xiv, 5, 7, 66–67, 101, 139
    Institute of (Australia), 115
    Landscape, 5
    Richardsonian Romanesque, 50
Architect and engineer (A&E) firms, 5, 7

Architectural history/historian, 5, 7, 20, 29,
    50–51, 92, 96, 139
Area(s) of potential effects (APE), 30–31,
    33–34, 37, 77, 80, 140
Army (United States), 13, 15, 18, 19n10, 58,
    76, 87, 110
Asia(n), 2, 117
Atlantic Ocean, 46
Auger, Chinese, 35, 127
Australia, 2, 55–56, 85, 111–17, 135
Austria, 128, 142n3
Authenticity, 59, 70

Bachelor's degree (BA), 6
Badagry, Lagos State (Nigeria), 135
Bars, 10
Behavior, human, 1, 7, 15, 113
Belief, human, 1, 3–4, 7, 9–10, 14, 29, 49, 57,
    80, 97
Belize, 117–125
    Book Industry Association, 118
    Defense Force, 124
    Electric Co., Ltd. (BECOL), 121
    History Association, 118
Belize City, 118–19
    Museum of, 118
Belmopan (Belize), 119
Benin (Nigeria), 135
Bickford, Anne, 113
Big Blue River Dam, 104–5
Bigtown, 17
Blinders, professional, 41–42
Bliss Center for the Performing Arts (Belize),
    118, 122
Border Patrol (United States), 87
Bowdler, Sandra, 113
Breaking Ground Heritage, 106, 107n13
British Commonwealth, 7, 117, 121
Budget(ing), 69, 89, 122
Buildings, 2–5, 7, 17–18, 28–31, 33, 35–37,
    40, 42–46, 48, 51, 56–57, 63–64,
    66–69, 80, 83, 87–89, 92–93, 97, 103,
    116, 119, 121, 123, 126, 133, 138, 140
    Historic, 5, 37, 66, 83, 93, 97, 103, 108,
        126, 138
    Survey, Historic American (HABS), 37, 39
Bulldozer, 53, 90, 95, 102
Bureaucracy, x, 7, 11, 18, 27, 54, 76, 94, 126,
    132
Burra Charter, 112–15, 117, 136n2, 136n7

Cahuilla Tribe, 9
California, xiii, 2, 5, 9, 44, 54, 64, 95, 104

Environmental Quality Act (CEQA), 2, 5,
    95
Canada, 55–56, 85, 120, 123
Capitalism/capitalist, xi, 12, 95, 128
Caracol, 123
Caribbean, 124
Chicken grit, xii, 141
Chicken houses, 67
China, 35, 55–56, 107n14, 125–27, 141
Ch'u'itnu River, 9, 58
Citizen(s), 3, 8, 12, 47, 81, 95, 122–23, 140–41
Clearing construction projects, 14, 132
Client(s), 6, 11–12, 15–16, 24–29, 31, 33, 37,
    41–42, 52–53, 62, 65, 70–71, 76–77,
    82, 84, 91, 97–98, 109, 131, 135,
    140–41
Climate crisis, 102–3, 108–9
Coast Guard, United States, 15, 87
Colombia, 59n7
Colorado River, 9
Community/ies, 5–11, 13, 15, 28–29, 31–32,
    36, 40, 44–45, 49–51, 54–55, 70,
    77–78, 82–83, 89, 96, 102–3, 116–19,
    121, 124–25, 131, 135, 138–40
Compensation, 4, 73–74, 83
Compliance, xiv, xv, 13–14, 16, 22, 100, 116,
    129–30, 132, 140
Confidentiality, 97
Congress
    National People's (China), 126
    United States, xiii–xiv, 37, 47, 80, 88, 143
Constitution, United States, 45, 143
Construction, 2, 4–5, 46, 50, 53, 64, 67, 87, 95,
    99, 121, 130, 134–35
Consultant(s), 5–6, 9, 16, 24, 30, 48, 55, 80,
    94, 112, 131
Consultation, 14, 24–28, 31–32, 35–38, 52,
    55, 63, 67, 69–71, 73–86, 88–90, 93, 96,
    98, 101–2, 116–17, 132, 134, 136n8,
    139–40, 146
    Definitions of, 25
    Guidelines for, 25–26
    Time limits on, 26, 77
Consultation and Cultural Heritage (Nissley
    and King), 79, 81
Contexts, historic, 55
Contracting Officer's Technical Representa-
    tive (COTR), 94
Corporations, Native, in Alaska, xii
Corps of Engineers, United States Army, 13,
    15, 17–18
Council on Environmental Quality (CEQ),
    13, 73, 145

Court(s), 12, 16, 31, 46, 54, 60, 85, 97–98, 101, 104–5, 107, 140
Crown corporation, 123
Cultural geographer, 9
Cultural heritage, 3, 26, 29, 39, 58, 76, 101, 111, 117–19, 122, 124–26, 128–29, 131–33, 137, 139, 145
  Intangible, 28–29, 31–32, 34, 36, 39, 57–58, 70–71, 117–19, 123–24, 139, 144–45
Cultural Preservation, Ambassador's Fund for (United States), 122
Cultural relics departments (China), 126
Cultural resource(s)
  Defined, 1, 3–4
  Ownership of, 28, 35, 69, 116, 118–19, 122–23, 126, 128–29, 132–33, 141
  See also heritage
Cultural Resource Laws and Practice (King), 53
Cultural Resource Management (CRM)
  Activism in, 103–4
  In Australia, 111–17
  As a business, 5–6, 12, 22, 27, 90–91, 99–100, 105–6, 109
  Assessing adverse effects in, 62–71
  Background research in, 31–34, 36–37, 52, 55, 62, 88–90, 132
  In Belize and Central America, 117–25
  Bias in, 41–42, 45, 47, 105n3, 113
  Bottom lines in, 138
  In China, 125–27
  Clients in, 11–12
  Communities in, 7–11
  Companies/industry, ix, 5–6, 58, 66, 101, 104, 127, 133, 132–33
  Consultation/negotiation in, 24–28
  Defined, 1–4
  Disasters and, 101–3
  In Europe, 127–33
  Evaluation in, 40–58
  Future for, 139–41
  Going to court in, 104–5
  In government agencies, 16–18
  In historical perspective, 1–7
  Identification in, 28–37
  Keeping secrets in, 96–99
  In land and building management, 87–95
  Legal underpinnings of, 142–46
  Monitoring as, 95–96
  In Nigeria, 133–35
  Non-centralized regime for, 141
  Non-development-related, 130
  Origins of, 1–2

  Parks and, 103
  Purposes of, 3–4
  Regulators in, 13–16
  Resolving adverse effects as, 72–85
  Studies as parts of, 89–95
  Subjectivity in, 11, 30, 41, 75, 97
  Who does it, 4–7, 111–14, 129–30
Culture, defined, 1
Culture, Ministry of, xiii
Culvert, 8, 16–17
Curation, 83, 110, 120, 122
Curtis Jenny, 46
Customary beliefs, 1, 3–4, 7
Customer Relations Management (CRM), 1

Daesh, 101, 107n1
Davis-King, Shelly, 10–11
Defense, Department of (DOD, United States), xii, xv, 23, 27, 87, 97, 133
Demolition, 4, 66, 82
Dendrogylphs, 102, 107n2
Developer/ment (of land), xiv, 2, 12–13, 44, 56–57, 66, 85, 96, 104, 112, 115, 120–21, 124–25, 128–32
Dictionary, Merriam-Webster, 1, 7, 25, 43, 49, 65, 73
Disasters, 101–3
District of Columbia, 13
District(s), 2, 17, 39, 42, 44–46, 48, 51, 56–57, 64, 119, 140
  In Belize, 119
  Discontiguous, 45–46
Doctorate (PhD), 6, 119–20
Documentation, 27–28, 37, 41, 49, 52, 58, 79–85, 133, 140
Dugong(s), 54, 59n2, 60, 76, 78
Dugong v. Rumsfeld, 54, 59n2, 60
Duke University, 9

Earhart, Amelia, 46
Earthwalker, 35
East Indian Council (Belize), 118
Edo State (Nigeria), 135
Education and Culture, Ministry of (Belize), 118, 123
Effects, 14, 30, 62–76
  Adverse, criteria of, 62–76, 78–81, 83–86, 89, 101, 131–32, 139
  Avoiding, 71, 73–75, 81, 83, 85, 95, 139
  Cumulative, 30, 33, 64–65, 70, 80, 139
    Definition of, 65
  Direct, 30, 33, 63–64, 80, 139–40
  Indirect, 30, 33, 63–64, 80, 139

Effects (*cont.*)
    Minimizing, 4, 73–75, 83, 108, 139
    Mitigating. *See* mitigation
    Resolving, 72–85
Energy, Department of (DOE, United States),
        xii, 15, 87
Engineer/engineering, xiii, 5, 13, 15, 17, 25,
        36–37, 46, 51, 84, 101
    Record, Historic American (HAER), 37, 39
Environment, 2, 4, 13, 24, 31, 45, 70, 77, 91,
        114, 120, 136nn6–8, 138, 142n3
    Department of (Belize), 120
    Social, 91–92
Environmental
    Impact Assessment (EIA), 4–6, 9, 16, 75,
        87, 104, 120, 128–29, 131, 137
            Companies/industry, 4–6, 9, 16, 104
    Justice, 13, 45, 107
    Protection Agency (EPA, United States),
        13
    Protection and Biodiversity Conservation
        Act 1999 (Australia), 114
Erosion, coastal, 89, 102–3, 106
Ethnography/er, 5, 9, 10–11, 49–50, 92, 138
Europe/an, x, 2, 56–57, 85, 111, 115, 121–22,
        127–37, 141
    Convention for the Protection of the
        Archaeological Heritage, 130, 137n15
    Council of, 131
            Framework Convention on the
            Value of Cultural Heritage for
            Society, 131, 137n16
European Union, 57, 122, 129, 137
    Directive on EIA, 137n14
Evaluation, 40–58
    Versus listing, 41

Federal
    Capital Territory (Nigeria), 134
    Emergency Management Agency (FEMA,
        United States), 102–3, 107–8
    Energy Regulatory Commission (FERC,
        United States), 14–15
Federal Planning and Historic Places (King), 81
Fires, 102
Fish and Wildlife Service (United States), 13,
        15, 87
Folklife/lore/ways, 29, 57, 68
Forest Service (United States), 8, 15–16, 87
Fort Polk, 58
Fowler, Senator Wyche, 99n1
France, 128
Frog effigy, 10

Funding, sources of, xiii–xv, 12–14, 59n12,
        84, 89, 116, 119–20, 122, 126–27,
        129–30, 135

General Services Administration (GSA,
        United States), 87
Geography, 5, 44–45, 120–21
Germany, 128
Getting Past No (Ury), 79
Getting to Yes (Fisher and Ury), 79
Golden Gate Bridge, 41
Government/law, local, xii–xiv, 14, 24, 35, 39,
        42, 48, 69, 76, 115–16, 126
Government/law, state, xii, 13–14, 48, 59n7,
        69, 98, 114–16, 129, 130–31, 138, 143
Grants, xiv, 13, 116, 122–23, 130, 144–45
Gray, Jay, 6
Great Archaeological Sites (*Da yizhi*, China),
        127
Great Lizard, 35
Great Wall (China), 126
Guam, xi, xiii
Guatemala, 123–24

Harrington, John Peabody, 11
Heritage, ix, 3, 15, 20, 22, 29, 31–32, 37, 39,
        56–61, 76, 78, 101–2, 106, 111–33,
        136–39, 142n3, 144–45
    Built, 51, 66, 127
    Cultural, ix, 3, 111
    Ethnic, 38, 44, 56, 118–19
    Intangible, 28–29, 31–32, 34, 36, 39,
        57–58, 61, 70–71, 117–19, 123–24,
        137n13, 139, 144–45
    Management, 112–13, 115–17, 123, 128
    Protection, ix, 3
    Resource management, 3
    Tangible, 28–29, 34, 58, 71, 139
    See also cultural resources
Heritage Sites with National Significance,
        Register of (*Quanguo zhongdian
        wenwu baohu danwei*, China), 126
Highway A–106, 17
Historian/history, ix, xiii, 5–7, 20–21, 31–32,
        36, 41, 45, 48–50, 55, 60, 78, 92, 96,
        102, 110, 112, 118–19, 121–22, 124,
        126, 136, 138–40
    Architectural, 5, 7, 20, 29, 36, 42, 50–51,
        92, 96, 112, 139
    Art, 42
    Engineering, 36
    Landscape, 5
    Oral, 5, 21, 48, 50, 113
    Public, 7, 21

Historical
  Architect/ture. *See* architect(ure),
    historical
  Research, Department of (Honduras), 123
  Resources Ministry, 14
Historic place/property, 2–4, 13, 15, 30–31,
    33, 37, 39, 42, 60, 63–66, 70, 72–73, 77,
    86, 88, 107, 145
  Categories (United States), 42–47
  Integrity of, 5, 47, 59, 63–64, 68, 70, 77,
    113
  Significance of, 9, 14, 22, 36–37, 40–41,
    46–50, 60, 68–69, 77, 103, 113–14,
    115–16, 126–27, 128, 133, 136n3
    Levels of, 47–48, 116, 126, 128,
      132–33, 70
Historic preservation, ix, xiii–xiv, 2, 7–8,
    13–14, 19–23, 25, 38, 44, 55, 63, 67,
    72, 76–77, 86, 99–100, 102–3, 109–10,
    139, 145–46
Historic Shipwrecks Act 1976 (Australia), 114
Homeland Security, Department of (DHS,
    United States), 87–88
Honduras, 123
Horses, wild, 9, 58, 76, 78
Houses of Culture (HOC, Belize), 118–19
Hydrogrow Irrigation, 17

Ibadan, University of (Nigeria), 134
ICAHM (International Committee on
    Archaeological Heritage Manage-
    ment), 57
ICOMOS (International Council on Monu-
    ments and Sites), 57, 112, 117,
    136nn1–2
ICUN (International Union for Conservation
    of Nature), 57
India(n), 8, 56, 59n7
  East, 117
Indian tribe. *See* Tribe, Indian. *See also* Native
    American
Indigenous, 8, 22, 29, 34, 44–45, 49–51, 55,
    57, 64, 74, 77–78, 85, 95, 112–15, 117,
    135, 136n1, 136n5, 136n9, 136n144
Institute of Archaeology (China), 127
Institute of Archaeology (IA, Belize), 117–22,
    124
Institute of Creative Arts (ICA, Belize), 117–
    18
Institute of Social and Cultural Research
    (ISCR, Belize), 118–19
Instituto de Antropología e Historia (IDAEH,
    Guatemala), 123

Instituto de Bellas Artes (Guatemala), 123
Instituto Hondureño de Antropología e His-
    toria (IDEA, Honduras), 123
Interdisciplinary character of CRM, 5, 9, 42,
    138
Interior, Department/Secretary of, xii, 39, 54,
    66, 72, 77, 86–88, 100, 145
Internet, 55, 124
Italy, 128

Japan, 54–55
Judge(s), 3

Kansas, 46
Karl, Raimund, writings of, 141
Karuk Tribe, 64
Katamin, 64
Kentucky, 9
Kick-the-can syndrome, 79–80, 83
Kiribati, 103
Klamath River, 9
Klingon, 96
Knowledge, human, 1, 7–8, 36, 39, 92, 113
  Traditional ecological (TEK), 36, 39

Land Management, Bureau of (BLM, United
    States), 15, 87
Lands, submerged, xi–xiii, 4
Landscape(s), 5, 17–18, 32–34, 37, 39, 44,
    46, 51–52, 56, 58, 60, 63, 83–84, 112,
    133, 138
  Architect(ure), 5, 51–52
  Cultural, 18, 32–33, 51–52, 58, 60, 138,
    140
  Designed, 83
  Historic American Survey (HALS), 37,
    39
  History, 5
  Political, 56
Landscaping, 83
Language, 10, 18, 25, 29, 31–32, 45, 57–58, 64,
    67, 69–70, 74–75, 80, 82, 138
  As cultural resource, 29, 31, 57–58, 70,
    138
Law(s)/legislation
  Of Belize, Subsidiary, 117
  Cultural heritage/resource, xi–xv, 1–4,
    6, 8, 10–13, 16–17, 19, 24, 26–30, 33,
    39, 48, 53–54, 59nn1–3, 60, 62–63,
    66, 70–72, 73, 75–76, 78, 84, 88, 93,
    96–97, 106, 109, 111, 114–16, 117–18,
    122–23, 125–26, 128–29, 132–33, 134,
    139, 142n3, 143–46

Law(s)/legislation (*cont.*)
  Environmental, xi–xv, 1–3, 8, 10–12,
    16–17, 19, 24, 27–28, 30, 33, 54, 76, 78,
    93, 109, 115, 143–46
  International, 57, 76, 96, 143–45
  Local, 14, 35, 69, 76, 96
  Of the People's Repub-
    lic of China in the Protection of Cul-
    tural Relics, the, 126
  State, 14, 69, 76, 96
  Tribal, 14, 76, 96
Lawyer(s), 76, 78, 90, 104–5
Limited liability company (LLC), 91
List/inventory/register/schedule, 2–3, 13, 15,
    31, 39–48, 50–61, 63–64, 75, 88–89,
    96, 99, 101, 113–15, 117–18, 121–22,
    125–27, 129, 131–32, 136n3, 139–40,
    144, 145
Litigation, litigators, 12, 45–46, 97–98, 109
Littleburg, 17
Lockheed Vega, 46
Looters/ing, 57, 121, 124–25, 131
Louisiana, 9, 58, 76
Luiseño Tribe, 9

Macal River Valley, Belize, 120–21
Maldives, 103
Management
  And Budget, Office of (OMB, United
    States), 93
  Of buildings, 87–88
  Definition, 1
  Of land, 15–17, 41, 87–99, 131
Maryland, 76
Marshall Islands, 103
Massachusetts, 117
Master's degree, 6, 120
Materials, material traits, 1, 3–4, 7, 46–47,
    63–64, 67, 82–83, 117
Mattson, Hannah, 6
Maya, 117, 119, 121, 123–24
  Councils (Belize), 119
  Mundo, 124
McGhee, Fred, 31
Memorandum of Agreement (MOA). *See*
  Agreement
Memorandum of Understanding (MOU)
  Tri-National Protected Areas and Conser-
    vation (Belize, Mexico, Guatemala),
    124–25
Mephitophobics, 68
Mexico, 124–25
Micronesia, 9, 103

Midden, 44, 67
Mitigation, 3–4, 67, 71, 73–75, 79–89, 95–96,
    120–21, 139
  Definitions, 73–75
  Doing archaeology as, 74, 82–83, 120–21
Miwok, 10
Money for CRM, xiii–xv, 11–13, 15, 48, 55,
    59n12, 69, 76, 84, 88–89, 93–94, 96,
    99, 104, 107, 116, 118–19, 122, 126–27,
    129–30, 140
  Year-end, 93–94
Monitor(ing), 56, 87, 95–96, 99, 101, 103, 108,
    116, 124–25
Monument(s), 56, 59n9, 119–21, 123, 132–34,
    136n2
Moss-Bennett Act. *See* AHPA
Mountain Valley Pipeline, 58
Munsell soil color chart, 35
Museum(s), 14, 47, 54, 84, 94, 101, 103, 118–
    19, 122–23, 133–34, 146
  Of Belize (MOB), 118–19, 122–23
  National, 14, 119

Nation, First, 79. *See also* Indian, Indigenous,
    Native American, Tribe
National Archaeological Parks (*Guojia kaogu
    yizhi gongyuan*, China), 127
National Archives and Records Service
    (Belize), 119
National Bureau of Cultural Relics (China),
    125, 127
National Commission for Monuments and
    Museums (Nigeria), 134
National Environmental Policy Act (NEPA,
    United States), 2–3, 5, 8, 10, 13, 17, 19,
    24, 27, 30, 33, 36, 54, 57, 64, 73–75, 87,
    93, 96, 106, 109, 145
National Garifuna Council (Belize), 119
National Heritage List (Australia), 114
National Historic Preservation Act (NHPA,
    United States), xiii, 2–5, 8, 10, 13–19,
    22, 24–25, 27, 30, 33, 36, 42, 48, 54, 63,
    69, 71, 73–77, 79–81, 84, 86–89, 96,
    109, 139–40, 145–46
  Section 106, 2, 14–18, 22, 25, 27, 30,
    38, 48, 54, 63–64, 66, 69–71, 73–82,
    84–89, 92–93, 96, 139–140, 142n2,
    145
  Section 110, 88–89, 92–93, 100, 146
National Institute of Culture and History
    (NICH, Belize), 117–19, 121–24
National Kriol Council (Belize), 118
National Library System (Belize), 119

National Parks and Wildlife Act 1974 (New South Wales), 116
National Park Service (NPS, United States), xiv, 3, 13–15, 19, 21, 25, 39, 43–45, 54–55, 59n6, 60–61, 76, 87–87, 96, 99n1, 102–3, 107–108, 146
National Population Commission (Nigeria), 134
National Register of Historic Places (NRHP, United States), xiii, 2–3, 13, 15, 31, 40, 43–60, 62, 64, 88–89, 96, 99, 107, 139–40, 145
    Bulletins, etc., 54–55
    Criteria, 48–53
    Criteria considerations, 53–54
    Keeper of, 54
    Living things and, 54
    Nominations to, 13, 46–48, 55, 60, 88–89, 96, 101
National Trust (Australia), 115
National Trust (United Kingdom), 104, 107n4
National Trust for Historic Preservation (United States), 76, 99n1, 103, 107n3
Native American, 2, 9, 54, 74, 83, 86, 95, 104, 146
    Graves Protection and Repatriation Act (NAGPRA), 2, 54, 83, 86, 146
    Rights Fund (NARF), 104, 107n6
Native Hawaiian, 69, 146
Navy (United States), 68, 76, 87
Negotiating Across Cultures (Cohen), 79
Negotiation. *See* consultation
New South Wales, 115–17
New Zealand, 8, 55–56, 59n7, 107n2
Nibbly Knob, 31
Nissley, Claudia, 79, 81, 140, 142n2
Nixon, Richard, xiii, 48
"No agreement" cases, 84–85
Non-archaeological, 9, 17, 35, 40, 52, 79, 138
Non-built, 66
Non-compete clause, 98
Non-compliance, 140
Non-cultural, 24, 138
Non-disclosure agreement (NDA), 97–99, 107
Non-electronic, 121
Non-federal, xiv, 75
Non-governmental, xiv, 81, 94–95, 115, 124
    Organization (NGO), 115, 123–24
Non-human, 8, 59
Non-Indigenous/non-Native, 95, 117
Non-originalist, 45
Non-professional, 39
Non-profit, 127

Non-scholarly, 101
Non-state actors, 101
Non-statutory, 112–13, 115
Non-tribal, 81
Notes, Take Better, website, 81

Objectivity, 30, 41, 75, 97
Objects, 2, 39, 42, 44–48, 54, 56–57, 60, 64, 70, 80, 116, 119, 121–23, 125, 128, 133, 137n13
Ohio, 59n7
Ojibwe, 9
Okinawa, 9, 59n2, 60
Oregon, 76

Pacific Islands, 3, 56
Paleontology, 59n5
Palmyra, 101
Parker, Pat (Patricia L.), 10, 22, 59n6
Parliament(s), 85, 128
Parthenon, 41
Parties, consulting, 74, 81–82, 90
Peking University, 127
People's Republic of China, 125
    Standing Committee, National People's Congress, 126
    See also China
Permits, xiii, 13, 18, 19n6, 71, 81, 114–16, 118–22, 124, 129–30, 132–33
Planning, xiii–xiv, 3, 23, 39, 41, 48, 57, 81, 86, 96, 99, 107–9, 112, 115, 127–28, 130, 132–33, 136n5, 138n3, 139
Plans, management, 83, 113
Pleistocene, 88–89Pointypeak Mountain, 30
"Polluter pays" principle, 130
Portuguese-American, 10
Practice, professional, ix, xi, xiv, 8, 98
Preservation Commission, 14
Private sector, 5, 27, 94, 97, 112, 123, 130, 132
Properties, historic. *See* Historic place/ property
Property, private, xi–xiii, 69, 76, 88, 115–16, 118–20, 126–28, 141
Property owner/ship, xii, xiv, 3, 14, 28, 35, 46, 66, 69, 76, 78, 81, 88, 116, 118, 120, 123, 126, 128–29, 131–33, 141
Proposals, Request for (RFP), 90–91, 94–95, 99, 105–7
Public historians, 7, 21
Public houses (pubs), 10
Public involvement/participation, 8, 80, 91–92, 99
Puerto Rico, xi

Quechan tribe, 9
Queensland, University of, 112
Quotes, request for (RFQ), 90

Ramirez, Constance, 38n6
Records checks, 31–32
Redundancy, 52
Regulations/regulators, xiv, 2–3, 5–6, 8,
        12–19, 22–25, 27–30, 32, 35, 37, 45,
        47–48, 54, 60, 63–65, 70–76, 79–80,
        84–85, 90, 93–94, 96, 98–99, 101,
        105–6, 115, 117–18, 126, 131–32, 134,
        140–41, 143–46
    Federal Acquisition (FAR, United States),
        90, 99
    NEPA (United States), 27, 64, 74–75, 145
    NHPA Section 106 (United States), 2, 25,
        27, 30, 54, 63, 71, 74, 77, 84–85, 93,
        140, 146
    NRHP (United States, 48, 59nn3–4, 60
Rehabilitation, 66–67, 83, 107
Repatriation, 83, 86, 146
Research, 5–6, 17–18, 31–34, 36–37, 40, 42,
        47, 49, 52, 55, 62, 69, 82–83, 88–90,
        105, 112–13, 116, 118–24, 126–27,
        129, 132–33, 135, 140
    Background, 31–34, 36–37, 52, 55, 62,
        88–90, 132
    Interdisciplinary, 5, 13
Respect, 5, 8, 11, 26, 29, 36, 45, 50, 57, 70, 78,
        102, 105–6, 138–39, 141
Retrofit, seismic 101, 107–8
Rock art, 36, 38n10, 102
Roiling Rapids, 31
Rule, Golden, 11
Russia, xii, 56, 107n14

Scoping/scopes of work, 32–33, 36–37, 64, 77,
        89–90, 93–94, 132
Sea Cow, Cosmic, 52
Secrets, 96–99
Set-asides, 90–91
Shovel, Sally, 17
Shovel test pits/units, 35
Silk Road, Maritime (China) 126
Site(s), 2–4, 7, 17–18, 26, 28–29, 31–35, 40,
        42–49, 51–54, 56–57, 59–60, 64–67,
        69, 71, 79–80, 82–83, 88, 92–93,
        96–97, 101–4, 106, 108–9, 112–16,
        120–27, 129, 131–33, 136–38,
        140–41
Smells, 31, 33, 35, 38n6, 67, 83
Social forms, 1, 3, 7

Social Science(s)
    Chinese Academy of, 127
    School of, University of Queensland, 112
Sociologist, 9, 22
Spanish, 25, 117, 121
Species, endangered, 13, 18, 109
Standards and Guidelines (United States, Sec-
        retary of the Interior)
    For Federal Agency Historic Preservation
        Programs Pursuant to the National
        Historic Preservation Act, 25–26, 77,
        86, 100
    For the Treatment of Historic Properties
        (36 CFR part 68), 66–67, 72
State Historic Preservation Officer (SHPO),
        13–16, 18, 22–23, 31–32, 45, 55, 63, 71,
        75–76, 78, 80–82, 96, 102, 140, 145–46
    "Clearance" by, 14
    National Conference of, 99n1
State, United States Department of, xv
St. Peter's Basilica, 45
Structure(s), xiv, 2, 5, 9, 28, 36, 39, 42–48, 51,
        56–57, 64, 66, 69, 80, 83, 102, 108, 110,
        119, 123, 126, 137
    Historic, xiv, 5, 46–47, 64, 66, 83, 119
    Sacred, 99
    Of symbol, belief, and power, 9
Studies, 3, 17, 31, 87–98, 103, 108, 117, 120,
        124, 136n10
Survey
    Archaeological, 2, 31, 33–34, 56, 88–89,
        92, 102, 121, 123, 127, 129, 136
        Non-destructive, 129
            Shovel tests in, 35
            Transect, 34
    Historic American Buildings (HABS),
        37–39
    Historic American Landscapes (HALs), 37
    Non-archaeological, 34–39, 88–89, 92, 102
Survival International, 104, 107n8
Sustainable Preservation Initiative, 104,
        107n9
Syria, 101
System(s)
    Australian heritage, 112–16, 136
    Belief, 57
    Belizan, 117–123
    Bureaucratic, 11, 70
    Chinese, 126–29
    CRM/heritage, 56–57
    Elitist, 63
    European, 130–32
    For evaluation, 42–60

Improving, 139–41
Legal, 2, 5, 7, 71, 80, 87, 94
Mechanical, 5
Standard, 16, 35
Subsistence, 57
Values-based, 112–13
Swahilli, 25

Taj Mahal, 41
Taxes/tax code/tax breaks, xiv, 8, 24, 48, 55, 105
Texas, 9
Thoreau, Henry David, 138
Tourism, 120, 124–25, 133
Ministry of (Belize), 124
Ministry of Commerce and (Nigeria), 133
Traditional cultural place/property (TCP), 22, 49–50, 52, 59n6, 72
Traditional ecological knowledge (TEK), 36, 39
Transparency, 8
Trees/plants, 16, 32, 36, 44–46, 54, 58, 76, 102
Tribal Historic Preservation Officer (THPO), 13–14, 22, 76, 79, 81
Tribal trust lands, xii–xiii
Tribe/tribal, American Indian, xi–xiv, 9, 11, 13–15, 18, 24, 28, 38, 42, 59n6, 64, 69, 76, 81, 85, 95–97, 102–4, 139, 143–46
Trump, Donald, 53
Tuvalu, 103

"Unfind" things, 6, 131
United Kingdom, 55, 104, 106, 109, 120, 123, 128
United Nations, 57, 59n8, 143–44
Declaration on the Rights of Indigenous Peoples (UNDRIP), 57, 144
United Nations Educational, Scientific, and Cultural Organization (UNESCO), 29, 38–39, 57–61, 70, 108, 119, 122, 125, 143–45
Convention for the Safeguarding of the Intangile Cultural Heritage, 29, 57, 119, 144
Convention on the Means of Prohibiting and Preventing the Illicit Import, Export and Transfer of Ownership of Cultural Property, 125
World Heritage Convention/List, 31, 39, 57, 59–60, 114, 144
United States, ix–xv, 1–3, 5–9, 12–20, 22–28, 37–42, 44–45, 47–48, 50, 55–58, 60–63, 69–73, 75–76, 79–81, 84–87,

90, 93–97, 99–100, 102–3, 106, 108–10, 112–13, 118, 120–21, 125–28, 130, 132, 136n5, 139, 141, 143–46

Vegetation, 33, 35–36
Veryold Tribe, 79
Veterans, military, xii, 9, 87, 90–91, 106–7, 109–10
Conservation Corps, 106, 107n12
Curation Program, 106, 107n10
HistoriCorps, 106, 107n11
Veterans Affairs, United States Department of, xii, 87, 107
Virginia, 58, 76

Wandering River, 30
Wenwu management system (China), 125
Wikipedia, 13, 15, 20, 38, 107, 13
Workload, 16
World, center of the. *See* Katamin
World Bank, xiv, 7, 59
World Trade Center, New York, 53–54
World War II, 76
Worldwide cultural heritage/resource management, examples of, 111–37
Worldwide weblog, ix

Xunantunich, 123

Year, fiscal, xiii, 93, 99, 122

Zippyzap Energy, 17

CPSIA information can be obtained
at www.ICGtesting.com
Printed in the USA
JSHW011450130723
44708JS00003B/216

9 781789 206524